Recognizing and Rewarding Employees

Other titles in the Briefcase Series include:

A
Briefcase
Book

Recognizing
and Rewarding
Employees

R. Brayton Bowen

McGraw-Hill

New York San Francisco Washington, D.C. Auckland Bogotá
Caracas Lisbon London Madrid Mexico City Milan
Montreal New Delhi San Juan Singapore
Sydney Tokyo Toronto

McGraw-Hill

A Division of The **McGraw·Hill** *Companies*

1 2 3 4 5 6 7 8 9 0 AGM/AGM   0 9 8 7 6 5 4 3 2 1 0

ISBN 0-07-135617-7

This is a CWL Publishing Enterprises Book, *developed and produced for* McGraw-Hill by CWL Publishing Enterprises, *John A. Woods, President. For more information, contact CWL Publishing Enterprises, 3010 Irvington Way, Madison, WI 53713-3414, www.cwlpub.com. Robert Magnan served as editor. For McGraw-Hill, the sponsoring editor is Catherine Schwent, and the publisher is Jeffrey Krames.*

Printed and bound by Quebecor/Martinsburg.

This publication is designed to provide accurate and authoritative information in regard to the subject matter covered. It is sold with the understanding that neither the author nor the publisher is engaged in rendering legal, accounting, or other professional service. If legal advice or other expert assistance is required, the services of a competent professional person should be sought.
> *—From a Declaration of Principles jointly adopted by a Committee of the American Bar Association and a Committee of Publishers*

McGraw-Hill books are available at special quantity discounts to use as premiums and sale promotions, or for use in corporate training programs. For more information, please write to the Director of Special Sales, McGraw-Hill, 2 Penn Plaza, New York, NY 10128. Or contact your local bookstore.

This book is printed on recycled, acid-free paper containing a minimum of 50% recycled de-inked fiber.

Contents

Preface

Managing in today's complex environment is difficult. The unspoken psychological contract that defines the nature of the relationship between employers and employees continues to evolve. Employees are becoming increasingly "free" to move about—*within* as well as *between* organizations. Traditional boundaries of structure, time, location, and authority are blurring. Organizations striving to compete in a global economy are downsizing, merging, transforming, and migrating to newer forms of existence. Managers and non-managers alike are being challenged to do more with less, think "out of the box," and collaborate in new and innovative ways to achieve common objectives. The old traditions and systems are breaking down, and newer conventions are being tried to achieve breakthrough results.

In the midst of a new global wilderness are pioneers, common and uncommon travelers, managers, stewards, free agents, "virtual" workforces—all converging on some new promised land. If you plan to venture out and—better yet—survive, you'll need to know how to prepare yourself, what essential tools to take, what travel techniques and strategies to apply, and—ultimately—what "customs," "language," and "currency" will enable you to be conversant with the many people of varied interests and abilities you'll meet—and manage—along the way.

This is a book about a new frontier—the new workplace. It's a book about the needs and interests of the new workforce— epitomized by the "free agent/employee"—and the tools of *recognition* and *rewards*. You'll learn about:

- **The New Workplace**—its "free agent/employees"—their values, interests, and goals;

- **Work**—how to make it personally meaningful and more strategically aligned;
- **Motivation**—its source and what drives it;
- **Collaboration**—its importance, along with what promotes and hinders it;
- **Recognition**—its many forms and its powerful and empowering energy;
- **Rewards**—what's hot, what's not, and the difference between those that are *intrinsic* and *extrinsic*; and,
- **Stewardship**—how it differs from leadership and why it is so important in the new workplace.

This is a book about people *at work*—and, specifically, about recognition and rewards. It may surprise you. It may excite you. We hope it will inspire you. The insights we lend and the conclusions reached are intended to convey a message—namely, that travel into the new wilderness is not for the "casual" traveler or "half-a-measure" managers. Success will be predicated upon a deeper understanding and mastery of the subjects of motivation, recognition, and rewards.

Chapter Highlights

The subject of recognition and rewards is complex. Rewards have the power to punish as well as compensate. As a manager in the new workplace, you'll need to know how rewards work. We want you, our reader, to understand:

- The difference between rewarding and manipulating;
- The human nature of work and the relationship that exists between work and its performer/creators;
- The rewards of leadership and the illusory nature of power;
- How cultures shape desired outcomes and foster productivity and collaboration;
- Why recognition is a "whole person" experience;
- What reward systems move people and organizations closer to their goals; and

• How to foster responsibility and accountability naturally.

Special Features

The idea behind the books in the Briefcase Series is to give you practical information written in a friendly person-to-person style. The chapters are short, deal with tactical issues, and include lots of examples. They also feature numerous boxes designed to give you different types of specific information. Here's a description of the boxes you'll find in this book.

These boxes do just what they say: give you tips and tactics for being smart about recognition and rewards.

These boxes provide warnings for where things could go wrong when you're trying to recognize and reward employees.

Here you'll find how-to hints to effectively recognize and reward your employees.

Every subject has its special jargon and terms. These boxes provide definitions of these concepts.

Want to know how others have done it? Look for these boxes.

Here you'll find specific procedures you can follow when you want to recognize and reward an employee or team.

How can you make sure you won't make a mistake when managing? You can't, but these boxes will give you practical advice on how to minimize the possibility.

Acknowledgments

First, sincere thanks to my editor, John Woods, for his insight and constant recognition—commingled with an appropriate amount of prodding and patience—lots of patience. This work could not have happened without his leadership. And, thanks, too, to CWL editor, Bob Magnan, who is a master in a world of wannabes.

Next, to my good friend and mentor, Tom Brown, at Management General (@mgeneral.com), whose constant encouragement and unwavering confidence continue to prompt me to tell my truth. And to any number of clients, friends, CEOs, employees, colleagues, and fellow travelers, who have shared their experiences and their truths.

To my wife, Yolanda Smith, for her gentle patience and loving support, for her sharing and her truths, thank you. And, most especially, to my children, David, Christopher, and Catherine—for teaching me all about recognition and rewards, punishment and bribes, fatherhood and stewardship—you have my deepest love and lifelong gratitude. Continue to heal, to enlighten, and to re-create a world that so desperately needs your talents—as only you know how.

About the Author

R. Brayton Bowen is a senior consultant and president of The Howland Group. He has served as senior officer for Fortune 500 companies, including Federated Department Stores and Capital Holding Corporation (now AEGON) and has more than 25 years of corporate and consulting experience. He specializes in change management and is currently focusing on workplace issues, including anger in the workplace. Clients benefiting from his services include: Baxter Healthcare, Borg Warner, GTE, Upjohn Pharmaceutical, Bank of Tokyo, Washington Gas, Omnicare, Revlon, RyKrisp, and the U.S. Department of Housing and Urban Development.

He has been featured in several publications, including Harvard's *Management Update* and AMA's *Management Review* and has authored numerous management articles for national publications, including *Industry Week, Association Management,* and Berrett-Koehler's *At Work.* He has been a contributing instructional writer on the subject of systemwide leadership development for Seton Hall's Virtual University and is host and co-producer of the nationally distributed public radio documentary *Anger in the Workplace.* He holds both bachelor and master's degrees from Brown University. You can e-mail Brayton at RBBowen@howlandgroup.com or visit his Web site at www.howlandgroup.com. His address is The Howland Group, Waterfront Plaza, 325 West Main, Suite 1600, Louisville, KY 40202-4251. Telephone: (502) 585-3535; fax: (502) 589-3555.

Understanding the New Workplace

M anaging in today's complex work environment isn't as easy as it sounds. Of course, it never was; but any number of factors are making it even more challenging. It's the same with recognizing and rewarding employees.

The concept of *employee* is changing. No longer can we think of getting a job done with just *our* employees. We must now think in terms of all those who are needed to complete a mission—both within and outside of the traditional organizational boundaries. Similarly, we have to understand the importance of *recognition* in its broadest sense and the value of *reward systems*—in both monetary and non-monetary terms. Why? Because the nature of work itself is changing, and to do your job well as a manager you must first understand the nature of conditions both within and beyond your immediate control.

It used to be a manager could provide a performing employee with continuous employment—up to and including retirement—so long as the work was up to standards and attendance and punctuality were entirely satisfactory. But not any more. Mergers and acquisitions, corporate downsizings, "employment at will" policies, and other workplace practices are changing the notion of job permanence. Supplanted by practices of workplace flexibility,

1

improved profitability, and worker "disposability," workplace loyalty and permanent employment are concepts of the past.

It used to be a manager could promise employees "a day's pay for a day's work." But not any more. Increased performance demands have raised the bar on productivity to more than a day's work for a day's pay. Even a "day" may be *less* than eight hours, as the push for part-time and temporary workers increases. And what might have been acceptable output for both full- and part-time schedules is no longer.

It used to be incentive plans, like "piecework" schemes or sales "spiffs," were thought to motivate or incite workers to improve production or sell more of one type of goods over others. But not any more. Such plans have been dropped, modified, or replaced, as we seek to find better ways to influence behavior by recognizing and rewarding employees, especially in the context of high turnover rates and critical shortages of labor.

Indeed, the landscape is changing rapidly. Many of the old tools and promises—such as continuous employment, a guaranteed wage base, and traditional incentive plans—cannot be used in today's work environment as they once were. They're just not applicable. And, if the truth were known, some were never really all that effective to begin with.

So we'll begin by taking a look at how the workplace is changing. And then, in this and the chapters that follow, we'll identify what you as a manager need to know if you're to be successful in influencing others, especially with regard to the use of recognition and rewards. Some of the issues we'll discuss are extremely complex. Indeed, the answers may not be entirely evident, but you will come to know why recognizing and rewarding employees effectively is so important. In Chapters 2 and 8, we'll look at *why* so many approaches have failed in the past and which approaches tend to work better. Most important, we'll discuss how and what *you* can do to make a difference.

Today's workplace is one where no one expects permanence; employees must constantly prove their worth and "doing more with less" is the mantra for any number of organizations. Understandably, the resulting condition can leave employees

> ## Recognize the Signs of the Times
> Approach your job of managing by acknowledging today's reality:
> **Smart Managing**
> - It's a seller's market. Worker mobility is in. Permanent employment is out.
> - Building personal reputation is in. Workplace loyalty is out.
> - Staffing flexibility is in. Traditional organizational structures are out.
> - Reward and recognition systems that build individual and organizational esteem are in. Incentives that devalue human intelligence are out.
> - Flexible organization structures and collaborative relationships are in. Workers and work structures as we've known them are out.

feeling less valued and less rewarded than ever before. And yet, reward and recognition, as we'll see, are the very factors that can most influence worker attitude, productivity, and organizational competitiveness—not only with respect to selling and servicing customers but also with respect to attracting and retaining valued human resources.

Moving at the Speed of Change

One of the most prominent characteristics of today's workplace is change. And it's clear that the rate of change is accelerating. Competitive factors, new technology, and the press for increased returns have prompted many organizations to diversify their people resources. Full-time workforces have been augmented by a cadre of part-time and temporary resources. Whole departments are being outsourced to suppliers specializing in specific functions, with employees doing work for you, but being paid by someone else. In search of cheaper labor to produce goods and provide services to existing and new markets, companies have "globalized." Yet, the process for managing such organizations on a worldwide basis has become increasingly complex. And with the diversity of cultures, work ethics, and personal values, the task of recognizing and rewarding, not only employees but also all those beyond the traditional organizational boundaries who work with us has become increasingly complicated.

To promote faster response times to marketplace demands, many organizations are transforming their traditional, monolithic organization structures of "boxes and lines" into more team-based designs, where decision making is more decentralized and, therefore, less susceptible to burdensome time delays due to unwieldy approval processes.

Moreover, to ensure continuous improvement and ongoing adaptability, organizational members are being taught the skills of continuous reengineering and process improvement. In a word, organizations are continuously reinventing themselves through knowledgeable and responsive organizational members charged with making a difference.

Technology has done much to speed the process of doing business. But here too, "change" is the watchword. Computer hardware and software are mostly obsolete within months after release. Technical skills and competencies have to be renewed and updated constantly to keep up with advances in technology. And anyone without some computer literacy is virtually a dinosaur in today's environment.

With emphasis on short-term results and maximum flexibility, much of our workplace processes and thinking have turned to "just in time," e.g., just-in-time manufacturing, just-in-time

Skills That Matter in Today's Environment

Smart Managing   Look for examples of these skills; it's appropriate to recognize and reward them in today's environment:

- Continuous learning.
- Interpersonal effectiveness, i.e., teamwork.
- Creative problem solving.
- Ability to produce desired outcomes.
- Customer awareness and responsiveness.
- Professional competence.
- Technical ability, including computer literacy.
- Ability to "multi-task," i.e., perform several activities concurrently.
- Adaptability, e.g., to new assignments or different contexts.
- A "mission" perspective, i.e., recognizing what "we" are in business to do.
- Ethical behavior, i.e., principles and behaviors that promote honesty and integrity in individual and organizational relationships.

inventories, just-in-time services. Of course, the ability to provide such results depends upon a high degree of planning and forecasting—and incredible responsiveness—to ensure success.

Certainly, "time is money" and cutting time out of business operations saves on inventories, labor, and the cost of doing business. So, what's the one thing you can count on in the future? You guessed it: more change—and step on it!

Doing More with Less

Corporate America is downsizing at the rate of 600,000 to 700,000 jobs a year. Hardly a week goes by without some news of layoffs and job loss due to workforce restructuring. As workers are displaced, those remaining must deal with increased workloads and fewer coworkers. Consequently, stress builds and frustration increases. But, the push for greater profitability and improved production is reality, and so too is the demand to "do more with less." Managers are often caught in the middle.

Moreover, the nation's median age was 25 in the 1960s, and today more than half the workforce is older than 35. By the middle of the next century, reports Beverly Goldberg of the Century Foundation, a New York-based think tank, there will be more Americans in their 70s than in their teens. Nowhere will the effects be more noticeable than in the workplace. Yet few companies are preparing for the prospect of massive retirements beginning in the next 10 years. Managers need to rethink their relationship with older workers, as we'll discuss in Chapter

---

Reaching the Flash Point!   ⚠ CAUTION! ⚠

Don't make the mistake this supervisor did at a printing company that continuously demanded increased levels of productivity, while simultaneously reducing its workforce. Under constant threat of job loss and even plant closing, the union petitioned management to "ease up" by addressing individual worker needs. The situation erupted when a pressman was refused a reasonable accommodation by his supervisor. The refusal led to a shooting rampage by the employee that left 13 coworkers injured and eight others dead. Witnesses conjectured, "Had his supervisor responded to his need, it might never have happened." Extreme? Yes. But it happens.

6. The graying of America is a factor that threatens to exacerbate the condition of "doing more with less," and it will inflict extreme hardship on those remaining in the workplace if current social contracts and management attitudes are left unaltered.

The challenge for discerning managers becomes one of knowing how to improve productivity, profitability, *and* performance in constructive ways—particularly in the context of having to do more with less. Chapters 4, 5, and 6 will reveal how you can improve your personal impact on performance, while influencing the behavior of others. Indeed, failure to recognize and *respond* to the needs of employees—as more than one manager has discovered—can be costly, even disastrous. Confronted with the pressures to do more with less, some workplaces have reached and even surpassed the boiling point.

Free Agents

It used to be that when we used the term "free agent," it generally was in reference to some sports figure who had earned the right to declare his or her availability to be wooed by another team—for a better contract. In today's world of work, "free agent" refers to a new class of worker—indeed, a new mindset.

Consider the makeup of your workforce. Many employees have experienced or witnessed the effects of downsizing, particularly those over 40 (the "boomers") who have been in the workforce for some period of time. Then there are the "Xers"—those in their mid-20s to early 30s who have been feeling alienated, disenchanted, even disenfranchised, due in large part to the difficulties they encountered in finding "good jobs" right out of school and to having witnessed the massive dislocations of older workers before them—parents, relatives, neighbors. Fast appearing on the screen are the "Generation Y" workers, those born between 1978 and 1988, who are focused on their own wants and needs. In a healthy economy, they spend upwards of $140 billion annually on stuff that ostensibly makes them feel good.

Whether boomer, Xer, or Generation Y, all employees realize the tenuous nature of continued employment. Let's face it: we all do. So, what makes the "free agent" tick? Well, it's much the

Free agent Someone who:
- Looks for opportunities in change.
- Accepts the insecurity of a job.
- Is more interested in challenging work than in job titles.
- Is continuously adding to a "portfolio of assets."
- Continuously looks for new opportunities to market.
- Chooses new projects carefully.
- Is always improving the ability to be a productive team member.
- Is committed to remaining a free agent for life.

Source: adapted from Susan B. Gould, Kerry J. Weiner, and Barbara R. Levin, *Free Agents: People and Organizations Creating a New Working Community* (San Francisco: Jossey-Bass Publishers, 1997), p. 151.

same stuff that makes you tick. Money and things are important, of course. But they also want:

- Assignments that increase their experience base, by building technical and/or professional knowledge that enhances their market worth. In other words, they want to be able to find another job quickly because of the value they're seen to bring to another situation.
- Work that's interesting, challenging, fun, and fulfilling.
- Flexible work environments that enable them to meet their personal life needs outside of work. "Psychic income," like *public* recognition, not just "in-house" acclaim, although that's important, too.
- Opportunity for a "piece of the action"—rewards that recognize their individual and group contributions as unique. A convenient "3.5% or 4% across the board" just doesn't cut it.
- Personal endorsements, particularly the kind that build self-esteem and market value.

Many of these factors apply to those outside the traditional organizational boundaries—the true free agents, i.e., contractors, consultants, and suppliers. Their financial success depends on getting favorable recognition from their clients. The organizations that fail to recognize good work run the risk of not attracting the best free agents. Concerned about reputation, those free agents who fear the harm of critical references, the damnation of "faint praise," or the inability to satisfy clients who enjoy the reputation of being the most difficult by withholding their support, will move to serve other clients who will better appreciate and more positively endorse their efforts.

Whether inside or outside the traditional organization boundaries, free agents see themselves as continuously "self-employed." As a consequence, building expertise, reputation, market worth, and personal networks are highly important factors when they seek and accept work assignments.

New Entrants into the Workforce

For some period of time the makeup of our workforce has been changing. More than 60% of American women are in the labor pool—almost twice as many as 50 years ago—bringing the mix to more than 45% of the workforce. And many are mothers of young children. On the other hand, the percentage of men in the workforce is declining. Approximately 70% of American men are in the workforce, compared with 85% some 50 years ago. Moreover, the decline of men age 55 and older has been most noticeable. Every year, slightly more than 1.5 million new workers are entering the job market—from many sources. Several groups are particularly noteworthy.

Welfare reform brought millions of former welfare recipients to the workplace in the late '90s. No longer able to rely on public monies to provide full income for personal and dependent care needs, many welfare recipients were compelled to seek full-time employment. With little or no previous work experience, these new and/or returning entrants have had to acquire skills to meet entry-level requirements and orient themselves to the spoken and unspoken rules of their new environments.

Some have openly expressed resentment at having to take jobs with incomes that barely meet or exceed the minimum federal income standards for poverty. In effect, they may have been better able to meet their financial needs under federal and state welfare programs than through gainful employment. Others have expressed satisfaction with feeling "productive" and "worthwhile," even though their financial worries are far from over.

Still other entrants into the workforce are recent graduates. But there's a difference in their educational experience. Some may have been students in institutions where conflict and violence claimed the lives of other students and of faculty. They may tend to be fearful and distrusting of institutions and organizational settings that claim to have responsibility for their welfare. Most young people are far more computer-literate than their predecessors, and many are interested in immediate gratification (especially with respect to material goods) and are quick to move on to other interests if bored by those at hand.

So, what's the significance of all this for those in leadership positions? Pay attention to your people. Develop a vision that addresses their wants and needs, as well as those of the organization. Spend time with them and get to know them as individuals. That may be the ultimate form of recognition in today's workplace—the lives of those around you, as well as your own, may well depend on it.

Immigrants represent another source of new entrants into the workplace. Traditionally, a melting pot for the world, the United States is now receiving some 500,000 legal immigrants over its borders annually, along with approximately 250,000 illegal entrants. Representing various cultures, values, and ethnic traditions, these new workers are enriching our environment with fresh ideas and new desires, while challenging the skills and abilities of traditional managers. Of course, not every manager views such diverse backgrounds, perspectives, and talents with open arms, but the fact is there's a lot of intellectual potential and raw energy to be harnessed for the good of all concerned. The tendency will

---

What Makes Them Tick?

TRICKS OF THE TRADE

Managing people can take a lot of time. The key is spending enough time in the right ways. Given the diverse interests, backgrounds, and abilities of your employees, find out what motivates each of them to come to work. What are their reasons for being there, for making money, for accepting this assignment, for enduring these hardships, and so forth? The answers to these questions will provide insight into the recognition and rewards that will mean the most to them as individuals.

be to suppress the new and different by emphasizing "the way we do things around here." In Chapter 3 we'll discuss the human nature of work and the importance of resisting this tendency.

Combative Cultures

As we begin the 21st century, every indication is that the workplace of the future will be somewhat volatile. All we have to do is pick up a newspaper or turn on the television to confirm that, in general, anger in society abounds. And our American culture thrives on a model of conflict—"the battle of the sexes," "the war on poverty," "the presidency under fire," etc. Popular TV programs are formatted along similar lines: "discussions" turn into shouting matches and talk shows promote conflict of the highest order, where violence can erupt on stage.

Whether in Paducah, KY, Littleton, CO, or Anywhere, USA, young people are becoming wary of institutional environments and organizational settings that claim to have responsibility for their welfare. Whatever the reasons behind the violence in institutions around the country or the motives of the teenage perpetrators, one key finding is that relatively little *attention* was paid to the perpetrators *before* the incidents. Parents, faculty, and other students seem to have spent little or no time really getting to know what was going on in their lives. They were generally excluded from social groups. And, professionals knowledgeable about such events affirm that the perpetrators were emotionally "neglected," "ignored," or "excluded" by those most able to develop meaningful relationships with them.

For students in our educational system who experience attacks or threats, whether directly or indirectly, there is little "future view," according to the experts. Instead, there is a sense of uncertainty about the future, even disillusionment and fear. Television and electronic games, in large part, have served as surrogate parents and baby sitters, but the stereotypical "power" figures generated by the electronic media have served as poor substitutes for reality. Nevertheless, their influence has left their mark.

Now bring that orientation or mindset to the world of work. Add the continuing drive for increased productivity and profitability and the uncertainty of work assignments, and you've got one mighty good chance for something to explode. Workplace homicide is the fastest growing category of murder in America today. Approximately 800 to 1,000 are reported annually. It's the number-one cause of death for women in the workplace and the number-two cause for men.

Most managers will be challenged to keep their cool and operate in a way that is totally open and honest. It's best to recognize the tensions that exist in your organization. Work to minimize them for your people. Acknowledge each of your employees and show that you appreciate their efforts. Often, just affirming "work is hard" is recognition enough to help people get through the most difficult of situations.

As we'll discuss in Chapter 5, building the right *culture* in your department or organization will go a long way toward creating the right context for recognizing and rewarding employees. Not everyone understands the importance of culture, and yet it is critical to the success of your business. All too often, culture is the forgotten element of business planning.

> **Culture** The way people have to behave to *fit* within an organization, the feeling and spirit and unwritten rules. You cannot impose a culture. It's a natural development according to circumstances and personal dynamics. But if you understand the people and the conditions, if you show that you care about your employees and are attentive to their environment, and if you model the behavior you want to encourage, then you can influence that culture.

Teams and Teamwork

As organizations grow larger and marketplace demands increase, traditional organization structures are transforming themselves into team-based systems. The benefits of these newer structures are well documented:

- Decision making is pushed closer to where it counts—at the point of contact with the customer.
- Response times are faster: bureaucratic delays are minimized or eliminated when higher-ups are not involved in every decision.

- Team members feel accountable and responsible, i.e., "empowered" to do the "right" thing.
- Teamwork requires and fosters excellent interpersonal skills, problem-solving ability, and involvement in the work to be done.
- Team-based structures require less supervision. Given the elimination of hundreds of thousands of middle management positions over the last 20 or so years, in particular, that's an especially important point.
- Team-based designs encourage continuous "reengineering" of work processes to increase productivity, improve quality, and maximize efficiency.
- Teams are more focused on the outcomes of the *group* rather than individual agendas.

Our list is a short one, but it's highly representative of the benefits of such structures.

And yet there is a serious risk in assuming there is only one right structure or structural approach for any organization. The reality is that just isn't so. Organizations differ in their purposes, their goals, and their processes, so it's natural that they also differ in their work structures.

The basic truth underlying all structural designs, however, is that more is accomplished out of order than out of chaos. The need for order and systematic pathways for achieving desired outcomes is at the heart of structure. The challenge lies in finding the right structure for accomplishing optimum results, consistently and continuously.

Let's Get Organized!

How often have you heard that expression? Few managers really take time to do just that. In a society that's driven to action, managers often seem committed to the approach of "Ready, Fire, Aim." Ask your employees, "What's working?" and "What's not working?" Listen to what they say about how the system sometimes fails to recognize their needs and those of the customers they serve—both internal and external to the organization. Then use the information you collect to help figure out what type of structure for your group would work most efficiently and effectively.

Listening

This book is about recognition and rewards. One of the ways you can effectively recognize employees is simply by listening to them. Hear what they have to say about the availability of information, about cooperation and communication, about collaboration and "turf" issues, about waiting times and response times, about who's "in" and who's "out," and how the system separates people or brings them together. If you really listen, you'll begin to see ways of opening up the channels of energy and enthusiasm. You'll begin to recognize the strengths and abilities of people and processes that will make a positive difference for you and for them.

Smart Managing

How do you know what structure is best for your organization or functional area? Look at the *strategy direction* of the enterprise and the needs of the *marketplace,* and then determine which *systems* bring out the best in each individual. In the past people were required to serve structures, usually hierarchies. Today, organizational structures take many shapes, with the most successful being those that make it easiest for employees to work together and continuously improve the organization's ability to serve customers.

Finding the right structure requires that you be flexible, that you seek and receive feedback from your employees, that you involve everyone, that you test designs, and that you implement the structures that work best. That's hard work!

Globalization

Globalization has certainly opened up new sources of labor at lower costs and new marketing opportunities for goods and services. But while cheaper labor has attracted many organizations to export entire bases of operation to other countries, their reliance on lower-cost operating and manufacturing systems provides only short-term competitive advantage at best. The reality is that unless a workforce can be readied to meet the highest standards of industry leaders around the world, a short-term strategy of "cheap labor" is destined to fail.

Consequently, as with any new opportunity, there are plenty of new challenges. And those challenges increase significantly when you add to the equation the variables of linguistic, cultural, ethical, and political differences.

Once again, we're faced with the need to determine the best way to recognize individual differences, preferences, skills, interests, and abilities and to bring them together in a constructive process that benefits all concerned. And you think you've got problems making things work in *one* company in *one* country! Well, you ain't seen nothing yet. Indeed, I would venture to say that, depending on the field you're in, your personal success depends on how well you are able to effect positive outcomes with real people—around the world—with real bottom-line impact. Seem a little overwhelming? It can be, but not if you focus on doing *your* best, with *your* people, in *your* area of responsibility, in *your* corner of the world.

Globalization presents many of the same challenges as the traditional work environment. The difference is that those presented within the "four walls" of one's department or organization are kicked up a notch—across organizational boundaries, political boundaries, and national boundaries. Yet, the objectives for a manager should be the same: to determine how to recognize individual differences, to overcome misunderstanding and resistance, and to work together to achieve common goals.

Taking the Show on the Road

For Example

A senior electrical engineer for a global manufacturing firm described a recent trip to Latin America, where the U.S. team met with representatives from the firm's operations in two Latin American countries. As the meeting progressed, it became increasingly apparent that the reps from one country were distrustful of the reps from the other. So, it became necessary for the U.S. team to assess the needs and concerns of each party before presenting a plan that was mutually acceptable to both. Once their concerns were acknowledged and addressed, the plan provided a blueprint that would foster "cautious" collaboration until such time as both could become more comfortable dealing with one another directly. The moral of the story? Before you can go running, it's often necessary to remove pebbles from your shoe. Time spent before the start of the heat will be well worth it in the long run. (Pun intended.)

Spans of Control

Traditional models of management theorized that a "typical" manager could supervise effectively from seven to nine individuals, and that, to do this well, he or she would have to plan, manage, and execute superbly. The model was built to capitalize on the notion of "centralized" decision making. In essence, the ratio allowed the manager just enough time to make decisions for his or her direct reports and to second-guess any judgments they made. In the age of empowerment and modern communication technology, such models are no longer accurate.

More contemporary theories of organization design suggest that the span of supervision for a manager can be much greater—in some cases 20 or more. Team-based organizational designs—where employees are grouped into work systems—permit even greater spans of supervision.

> **Span of control** The number of people a manager can effectively supervise in an organization with a traditional hierarchical structure. The concept is somewhat misleading, in that the concept of "control" is illusory: in reality, we can't control anyone; we can only influence their behavior. Still, the concept suggests that a manager who supervises so *few* employees will have time to get into almost any aspect of their business.

In team-based structures, both the social and technical skills of team members are integrated in such a way as to enhance "self-direction," mostly eliminating the need for scrutiny by a manager or supervisor. In such organizations, the role of the manager shifts from *making the right decisions* to *providing guidance and support to others* so they can make the right decisions.

Investing your management time, effort, and attention in this way is a significant way of "recognizing" employees for having the basic desire to do a good job and "rewarding" them by letting them do it!

Connectivity and the Virtual Workforce

As we move into the world of Workforce 21—with "own" employees, consultants, temporary and contract personnel, free agents, new entrants, global partners, and telecommuters working on-site, off-site, and halfway around the world—our work relationships will be very different. Electronic systems will transmit data, audio messages, and images via satellite, transoceanic cable, microwaves, telephone lines, etc.

Instead of investing in bricks and mortar to house employees in some traditional office or manufacturing complex, organizations are investing in communications systems that transport information and people—or at least their electronic presence—instantly to anywhere needed. Telecommuting is becoming more and more common. The notion of an entire workforce being all *physically* in one place is gasping if not dead. We are becoming a *virtual* world, a community of virtual workers, virtual managers, virtual businesses, and virtual customers. And, the "currency" that makes it all go around is the "currency" of *personal satisfaction*!

So, what does all this mean to you as a manager? Well, it means you're going to have to figure out very different and new ways to recognize and reward your virtual human resources. Indeed, the emphasis will be less on your personal style and more on the ways in which you choose to recognize and reward. Challenging? You bet!

But, that's not all bad. In fact, just as "control" was an illusion for so many managers in years gone by, many reward systems—built with the belief they "motivated"

> **Key Term**
>
> **Telecommuter** Employee who works from his or her home, connected electronically to the organization. It used to be we'd think of someone sitting at home, doing work for his or her employer, as recovering from an illness. Today, many businesses are run from the home, and still more are operated with a network of people "commuting" to and from work via electronic linkages. And, while telecommuting was considered new age thinking just a few short years ago, for many today it's an indispensable way of working.

employees to do one thing or another—were bogus. They were anything but motivating—and rarely were they significant drivers of improved performance.

As we move into the future, we will need to identify new ways of adding value—making a difference—at every level. And, finding ways to do that in the face of distance, time, and personal differences will be demanding. In an increasingly *virtual* world, the challenge is increasingly *real!*

Search for Meaning

To appreciate the nature of the task of managing in the years ahead, we must be honest in looking at the past. With the unprecedented dislocation of millions of workers due to downsizing and the elimination of hundreds of thousands of middle management positions over the last 20 years or more, the workplace is anything but joyful. Americans work more hours than people in any other nation in the world, and pressures to increase productivity continue to mount. According to Alan Briskin, author of *The Stirring of Soul in the Workplace* (San Francisco: Berrett-Koehler Publishers, 1998), "We've been strip mining the people resources within our organizations for years." Add to the equation the uncertainty of employment assignments, the dispirited state of new entrants into the workforce, and the changing work ethic. In place of the old employer-employee relationships, we are having to forge new social and workplace "contracts."

The good news is that workers are no longer able to hide behind a dependency on organizations to take care of them; the emergence of the "free agent" promises a new state of self-reliance and determinism for the individual. The bad news is that "individual caring" and "commitment" are no more. Like "strangers in the night," people—whether "own" or "leased"—and the organizations that contract for their services are not committed to lasting relationships.

To move organizations in the future, managers and leaders will need to rekindle the spirit of enterprise. As we speak, words like "soul" and "spirit" are being added to the lexicon of business terminology to address what's missing from the psyche of the workplace. In essence, we are embarking upon an era of searching for new meaning in the world of work.

So now, here's the challenge. How will you design work engagements that are *meaningful*—to both the individual and the organization? How will you recognize people in ways that will help delineate a new kind of loyalty? How will you enrich the lives of those engaged in the process of doing work? How and why will you reward people you don't even see, much less "own"?

Manager's Checklist for Chapter 1

❏ Many factors are contributing to a new workplace, with its changing values and differing goals. Managers need to find new ways for recognizing and rewarding new entrants to the workplace in the future.

❏ The potential for conflict and even violence will be greater than in the past. Smart managers will have to learn how to recognize the telltale signs and build relationships early in the game to help people work through their differences.

❏ Smart managers will appreciate everyone is different and will work to recognize and reward each person based on his or her general interests, skills, and abilities.

❏ Globalization will require managers to effect positive outcomes through people—sometimes around the world. More will depend on their ability to influence others and less on direct supervisory skills.

❏ With continued expansion and contraction of the workforce, managers and employees will need to find new meaning in what they do. Loyalty and allegiance to a single organization are concepts of the past. Instead, managers will have to appeal to a deeper sense of integrity and personal commitment to the expressive and creative process of being productive.

The Difference Between Bribes and Flattery, Recognition and Rewards

Working men and women expect to be paid for their services. What could be more fundamental to the employer/ employee relationship than that? *How* they're paid, *how much,* and *why* are aspects of the same premise.

In this chapter we will discuss the pros and cons of rewards in the workplace. We'll also explore why some approaches to compensation, specifically with respect to incentives, are more effective than others. And we'll examine the importance of recognition as a means to influencing constructive behaviors.

The use of incentives in the American workplace is nothing new, and in some organizations it's very big business. In highly bureaucratic organizations, where many levels of organization separate upper management and the "worker," incentives act like surrogate bosses. The assumption is that middle management doesn't necessarily understand the priorities of top management, and workers can't be trusted to produce without some

Key Term   **Reward** Something given or received in return for service. We all know the definition of "reward," but we may not appreciate the variety of work rewards. Rewards cover a broad range of "payment"—including base compensation, bonuses, stock options, cash, and cash equivalents. Incentives, in particular, are a special form of reward, intended to encourage, stimulate, or incite employees to produce a desired action or behavior.

form of enticement, such as piece rates based on pieces produced and production quotas achieved, commissions, shift differentials, premium pay, etc. But, all that is changing.

Accelerated by the flattening of organizations and the loss of supervisory positions due to downsizing and enhanced by our penchant as a culture for immediate gratification, the use of incentives has increased significantly in recent years. One study found that some 500,000 firms were using group incentive programs in 1991, compared with approximately 2,000 in 1945.*

Consider how deeply ingrained incentives are in our society. Remember when you were in grade school and the teacher put a smiley face on a paper you wrote or scribbled "nice job" across the top? The purpose, of course, was to recognize your accomplishment and encourage you to produce similar results in the future. Were you surprised the first time? Did you like the feedback? And do you remember when you may have repeated that same performance and *didn't* get the recognition, or when you went to another class with some other teacher who didn't provide such kudos? Rather disappointing, wasn't it?

Your employees are no different. Once you start the process of recognizing and rewarding, for whatever reason, the expectation will be more, more, *more*! It's human nature. And that's OK. How you go about the process as a manager and for what purpose will determine whether or not you're successful.

Of course, we've all received different forms of reward and recognition in our lives. Perhaps they've come as special privileges for good work in grade school, merit badges for scouting,

*Haig R. Nalbantian and Andrew Schotter, "Productivity Under Group Incentives: An Experimental Study," *American Economic Review*, 87:3, June 1997.

citations for community service, metals for military accomplishments, or prizes for competing successfully in organized games or events. For the most part, these rewards were based on a simple model of *quid pro quo.*

We have rewards in the workplace in the form of incentives, contests, bonuses, prizes, gift certificates, days off with pay, ... and the list goes on. Some companies go to extremes by designing very elaborate programs.

A Bird for All Seasons

A retail store owner decided to give Thanksgiving turkeys to all employees as "thanks" for their work and encouragement for the holidays ahead. It was a first! The employees were surprised—and so appreciative! Many expressed their personal gratitude. The owner repeated the gesture the following year, only to find some were a little displeased that the birds were no larger than those before. As two more seasons passed, turkeys became a morale problem. Eventually, the owner replaced the program with bonuses. And—you guessed it—in time, satisfaction turned again to displeasure.

One nationally recognized retail chain went so far as to create a full-time staff position to do nothing but develop rewards programs for all of its retail locations. People within the organization called this person a "manager of whoopee" in recognition of all the fun and excitement generated by her programs.

Another organization, recognized as a global giant in manufacturing and communication, encouraged managers throughout the system to reward employees with all kinds of special awards and cash payments. A highly elaborate administrative system was designed to budget and distribute funds according to business unit and levels of authority within each unit. Over time

---

Key Term

Quid pro quo Latin for "one thing in exchange for another." We're certainly familiar with this concept in business. "Come to work on time every day and you'll get a bonus for perfect attendance." "Treat the customer appropriately and you'll win a dinner for two at your favorite restaurant." The convention is intended to motivate certain behavior by providing a positive consequence.

What Works?

Smart Managing   A *Fortune* 100 company executive responsible for increasing sales studied the effect of several variables on sales growth—*product availability, pricing, advertising,* and *incentives for sales personnel.* After months of analysis, he found two factors were "statistically significant" drivers of sales growth: product *pricing* and *advertising.* While product availability and incentives appeared to have some correlation, they were not statistically significant. In-stock items could be substituted for unavailable goods, and customers could "tolerate" staff if the price was right. Sales incentives, *per se,* had no significant impact on sales growth, the study concluded.

the program became highly political, as managers vied for greater funding in order to appear most beneficent.

The underlying assumption behind many reward systems is that a "gift" will improve performance or generate some other desired outcome. And, the theory goes, if you give *more* of something, you'll get more in return.

Of course, that's not always the case. Not everyone will respond to incentives. Also productivity levels fall off at some point, no matter how well you compensate. The effect of any incentive depends mostly on the *recipient!* Gifts, in general, are seen as just that—something to be used, saved, or given away. In a business context, they may or may not be relevant to the individual or to the bottom line. Consider the two examples cited above. The retail chain was not able to produce better bottom-line results; indeed, for some time sales declined while sales of competitors continued to grow. And the global manufacturer scrapped the system-wide program of giveaways when its business began to deteriorate and Wall Street feared for its financial welfare. Fortunately, both companies continue to do business today, but their emphasis has turned more to providing good products and exceptional customer satisfaction.

Certainly, as a manager, you want to reward people for doing a good job. And, let's face it, we all enjoy pleasurable surprises and, especially, sincere appreciation for our efforts. But the challenge is to find the right rewards and reward systems for the right reasons. You have to decide whether the reward you're giving is intended to:

- Express appreciation
- Recognize value
- Provide encouragement
- Compensate for taking and sharing risk
- Alleviate hardship, e.g., working beyond normal boundaries, hours, etc.
- Provide choices
- Simply make things fun

Depending on where people are with respect to being able to satisfy their basic needs, rewards will be more or less important. Employees who are struggling to meet basic needs want recognition and rewards in the form of cash awards, i.e., extra income opportunities. Employees who are a little more comfortable will tend to seek rewards and recognition in the form of "satisfaction income," e.g., time off with pay, public appreciation, more interesting assignments. Savvy managers understand the importance of meeting the needs of their employees as well as those of the organization.

Smart managers recognize that rewards are not the answer to every problem.

- If there *is* a problem, determine first whether the appropriate solution is a reward or reward system. You may get the results you want, but end up paying for the consequences.
- Consider rewards more as expressions of appreciation and ways to recognize meaningful contributions to continuous improvement.
- Avoid situations where rewards are perceived as manipulative. Sure, people come to work because they need to make a living. That's a given! But they also want work that is satisfying, challenging, fun, engaging, personally fulfilling. If you begin to think of people as so many performers jumping through hoops and of rewards as the only means to getting them to jump, then you're heading

> **CAUTION!**
>
> ### Rewards Are Not Like Duct Tape
>
> The owner of a regional law firm complained that his lawyers were not answering phones. "That's how we get business! If they don't answer, we're in trouble." He considered implementing an incentive system. Asking for ideas, he got swift and painful feedback: "You pay us to produce! If we interrupt our client meetings to answer phones, we'll lose existing business." The owner thought he could fix the problem with incentives. What it required was structure. Having a receptionist or paralegal screen calls proved more cost-effective and a much better use of resources.

down the road to disappointment—for everyone concerned.

- Avoid the internal conflicts created by systems that promote "winners" and "losers." It's more advisable to give *group* rewards, to compensate individuals based on the performance of a unit, a team, or the organization as a whole.

Don't insult the intelligence of your employees: at some level we all want to do a good job. Instead, find ways to pique their interests—positively—and, in the process, look at the needs of the whole person, as we'll discuss in Chapter 6.

Punishing and Piquing

Rewards are powerful tools of management and can influence human behavior far more than personal style or personal effectiveness—although leadership style and effectiveness are important, as we'll see in Chapter 4. Moreover, rewards are like two-edged swords that can satisfy or dissatisfy employees and, in turn, enhance or detract from the attainment of desired results. To appreciate this concept, managers must first understand two principles of any payment system.

First, to work properly, the philosophy behind the system should be predicated on the *fair* and *equitable* distribution of payment for the production of goods and services. Indeed, most base compensation systems are designed to ensure both *internal equity* and *external competitiveness*. To achieve these ends, sophisticated pay schemes—using "points," "factors," and other variables—are frequently utilized, to ensure that employees are being appropriately compensated based primarily on *contribution* (time, effort, and attention) and *job worth* (relative importance of the job). To ensure that jobs are being competitively valued with respect to the marketplace, wage and salary surveys are conducted periodically, particularly with respect to "benchmark" positions, i.e., jobs for which there are readily recognized comparable positions in the marketplace. Moreover, these pay systems are usually tested to ensure they do not have some unlawful adverse impact on groups of individuals according to age, sex, race, or other legally protected attributes.

Second, rewards represent an extension of power. Just as power can be used to help or to hurt, so also can rewards. Just as power can be used to give or to take away, so also can rewards. Just as power can be fair or unjust, so also can rewards. And, just as power can be exercised *over* people or shared *with* people, so also can rewards. Power in reward systems manifests itself in various ways, particularly with respect to incentives or alternative pay programs:

- *Risk accommodation.* Smart managers know that rewards must be sufficient to offset employee concerns and any tendency to avoid reasonable risk.
- *Efficacy.* The reward must be sufficiently effective as to produce not only a desired result but also compensate suitably for personal sacrifice, accommodation, or hardship, e.g., time-and-a-half for overtime, compensatory time for extra time worked, etc.
- *Ethics.* Rewards should not encourage employees to violate ethical standards or statutory requirements. Sounds pretty obvious, right? But, check out how many times people and organizations are indicted for bribes, fraud, and other wrongdoing to obtain contracts or other results on which bonuses are based or jobs are staked.

Smart managers understand these principles and work to ensure that the reward systems for their employees are fair, equitable, appropriate, and competitive relative to the marketplace.

Beginning with the Industrial Revolution in England around 1760 and continuing well into the 20th century, workers were seen as parts of a complex social and economic "machine" and, therefore, subjects for control and mechanical manipulation. In the early 1900s, Frederick Taylor introduced the concept of "piece-rate" pay as a means to stimulate productivity and motivate low- or nonproducing workers to do more. People were assumed to be lazy and, therefore, in need of monitoring. The piece-rate pay system was a means for controlling the distribution of pay in relationship to the work produced. Workers were paid on the basis of tasks completed or pieces produced. The concept represented a model of power *over* people rather than *with* people and was never adopted broadly in American business, but some industries implemented such systems and continue to operate them even today.

The weakness inherent in such systems is the failure to recognize the human and operating variables that inevitably arise in such systems. Raw materials may not be plentiful or flow continuously through the system. Market demands for products can go down. Operating systems may not function properly. All are factors that invariably lead to adjusting and readjusting the system. If an incentive or reward program puts employees at risk to not earn sufficient compensation because of factors beyond their control, that system—no matter how great the incentives or rewards—can be seen as constituting, not reward or incentive, but *punishment.*

Most important from the perspective of the organization, such systems fail to incorporate the input and ideas for continuous improvement that come from the people expending the effort. Put simply, if you encourage your employees to pursue set objectives but not also to make suggestions for improving processes, you may miss some important opportunities.

Indirectly, employees on salary or hourly rates of pay know their performance is important, and failure to be productive could lead to job loss. But performance-based reward systems, such as those described above, provide immediate feedback with respect to more *current* performance. Therefore, enlightened managers attempt to use a blend of base compensation and incentives. This combination ensures some measure of financial stability for the employee while offering opportunity to augment earnings through increased performance.

There's a fine line between rewarding and punishing, fairness and exploitation. Savvy managers know that enlightened self-interest is the best motivation for design-

A Penny for Your Thoughts

In the middle of a high-tech, robotic manufacturing plant located in Georgetown, Kentucky, operated by Toyota Motor Manufacturing, stands an employee contribution—bicycles. An employee suggested that bicycles would be a faster means of getting around the plant than walking. Toyota pays for each and every employee idea that it implements—some 40,000 such ideas annually in plants around the world. It's a fine example of rewarding members for contributions that benefit the whole team.

ing a reward system. When considering any way to reward performance, they ask themselves, "Will it get me what I want by benefiting my employees rather than manipulating them?" Making rewards on the basis of appreciation is different from forcing people to respond to a system that frustrates and punishes. Regarding people as cogs in a machine is different from respecting them as valued assets. Recognizing and rewarding people in ways that are meaningful and encouraging is constructive rather than exploitative.

Some experts oppose incentives on the premise that they devalue human dignity and distract people from their primary task, as we'll discuss below. They see such systems as potentially corrupting, as if people could be bought for the right price, and degrading, as if they were being conditioned to "salivate at the bell" like Pavlov's dog. We maintain that rewards are powerfully important tools for managers and, when used properly, they enhance the working experience for all, while furthering the goals of the organization.

As a manager, you also need to reflect on the degree of risk associated with the reward program. If the program is to operate properly, if it is to influence people to stretch beyond their comfort zone, if it is to achieve congruence with personal and organizational objectives, the rewards must clearly outweigh the risks. This is a principle even the most ardent of entrepreneurs can embrace. If the business concept or financial deal is so outrageous as to place all of the resources of the entrepreneur at risk, the risk may simply be too large for the potential reward and the entrepreneur will back off. On the other hand, if the potential reward outweighs the risk and the plan objectives seem attainable, the entrepreneur will be more likely to proceed. The same principle holds true with your employees.

If you're having difficulty accepting this argument, then raise your hand if you've ever thought about winning the lottery—even if you don't buy tickets. The analogy is similar. Even those who don't buy tickets on a regular basis are sometimes inclined to do so, because the gain is so much larger than the initial investment. Of course, the reason why people don't buy more frequently is that winning the lottery is not realistically achievable, because of the enormous odds.

Similarly, premium pay, such as time-and-a-half or double time, is generally offered as an incentive or even recompense for working overtime or coming in on a non-workday or holiday—principally because employees are being asked to extend beyond their normal boundaries with respect to regular work hours, personal time, family time, and rest and recreation time. Even with such incentives in place, there's no guarantee employees will respond to the call just for money.

Of course, any asset in the extreme becomes a liability. If the intent behind a reward system tends toward manipulation, if employees do not perceive the system itself as congruent with respect to personal and organizational needs, if the system tends to appear one-sided as in placing all the risk on the employee or outside resource, or if the reward seems disproportionate to the size of the undertaking, then it doesn't make sense to use that reward system! Smart managers know the importance of *partnering* with their people, a principle that applies to reward and recognition systems as well. Consequently, programs of risk sharing, profit sharing, gainsharing, and even suggestion programs appear less manipulative and more cognizant of the levels of individual and organizational contributions.

Difficulty with some incentive systems arises when managers attempt to shortchange employees by carving out too big a piece of base compensation, putting the balance at risk, as a re-earnable component of the total package. Some element of re-earnable compensation is desirable, but too big a chunk can lead to employee anxiety, dissatisfaction, even turnover. Moreover, how and why some portion of compensation is re-earnable must be *reasonable* (it makes good business sense), *attainable, intelligible* (it's easy to understand), and *responsive* to employee interests.

Tipped employees, primarily in food service and entertainment, are in a special class. Their wages are often below the federal standard. The assumption is that tips from customers will make up the difference between the discounted base wage and the required federal minimum. In this instance the legal system aligns with business to construct a system of pay that may not be consistently equitable and that shifts the burden of risk to the employee. Managers wishing to retain employees will generally pay a higher base wage, or promote their business to build traffic, or merchandise their menu to ensure larger checks,

---

Incentive Systems

To develop effective incentive systems, start by defining what you want to achieve. Then, get input from employees: what would work for them? The best systems meet the following criteria:
- The rewards are fair for the effort and risk: appropriate recompense for appropriate contributions.
- The system is equitable for all employees.
- The rewards are competitive with similar rewards offered by other companies.
- The rewards are appropriate for the results expected.
- The system shows respect for employees as people.
- The rewards may be achieved with a realistic effort.
- Employees understand how the reward system works.

If the proposed system meets the listed criteria, try it out. Then evaluate the results and get feedback from employees. If there are any problems, make adjustments. Repeat this process until your reward system meets all the criteria.

or all of the above. In other words, smart managers value their employees and work in their best interests, knowing that the interests of the customer will be better served.

The Truth About Motivation

Motivation is truly an "inside" job. No one can make you do something against your will. You may do something you don't particularly want to do, but it won't be against your will. You may be confronted with some extremely hard choices, but what you decide to do ultimately is your decision. The same is true of your employees. As noted above, paying a premium to work overtime or to come in on a holiday may influence some to respond to the call, but not everyone will make the sacrifice if they decide something else is more important. The most a manager can do in that situation is to provide the incentive, recognizing that, just like a gift, it can be refused—and it may be unlawful to compel the employee to "accept the gift."

The problem with "incentive mania" is that it puts emphasis on *secondary* considerations for being in business, whereas the *primary* focus should be on providing quality products and services to a world deserving of the best we have to offer. Similarly, as human beings endowed with certain skills, interests, and abilities, we should be focusing on giving the best of what we have to offer—primarily for *our* satisfaction and personal fulfillment. If we do that first, we'll then have the energy, resources, and inclination to fulfill the needs of others. And managers should be giving their best to ensure everyone is aligned, supported, and committed in the process. By doing this we satisfy the ultimate recipients of our work, i.e., the customer and all other stakeholders in the process. This may sound idealistic, but it is a worthy goal.

We need to take the longer view, and yet everything in our society draws us, seduces us, incites us to focus on the immediate. The subliminal message is that somehow things will be easier and better, and we'll be happier if we just buy this gadget now, if we just convert these investments to this opportunity, if we just acquire whatever other, presumably more successful people already own. Of course, life is not that way: life is difficult.

Similarly, many corporations are focused on the short term: we need to make these numbers this quarter, we need to have this percentage increase in productivity, we need to produce this amount of profit or else. For publicly held corporations, missing a forecast by as little as a penny can result in a significant drop in stock price, as investors move to punish the company for missing its projections.

Some companies have elected to take the longer view—e.g., Toyota Motor Manufacturing, Southwest Airlines, Hewlett-Packard, Men's Wearhouse, ServiceMaster, and Mary Kay Cosmetics—by investing in people and "pro-people" practices. Such practices are paying dividends, as these companies consistently outperform the competition.

Savvy managers appreciate the sense of urgency with respect to getting immediate results, but their inclination in managing people is to take the longer-term view. By emphasizing "work as its own reward" and pride as a benefit that comes from having taken on difficult challenges, they are helping employees realize the fulfillment and satisfaction of a job well done. Indeed, recognition is an even more powerful tool than rewards, although both are closely linked.

By recognizing effort, accomplishments, ideas, individual abilities, talents, etc.—all the things others may take for granted—smart managers know they are influencing and encouraging their employees to stay motivated about their work. This is particularly important in today's environment of flatter organizations, where the old paradigm of advancement, *i.e.*, climbing the ladder of success, is being replaced by horizontal advancement, i.e., acquiring greater competence and increased market worth. Recognition, therefore, becomes a means for signaling advancement in the current sense.

So if motivation to do good work is an intrinsic quality, what place do rewards and recognition have in the workplace? Actually, they have a critically important one. Incentives have

> **⚠ CAUTION! ⚠**
>
> ### Throwing the Baby out with the Bath Water
>
> Some experts in motivation theory claim that "grades, stickers, and other ... inducements" rob individuals of the intrinsic motivation to learn, produce, and excel over the long term. Indeed, while short-term performance may be heightened, long-term performance actually worsens. Eventually, the prize turkey just isn't big enough, and the rewards become more of a hindrance than help. Productivity declines and managers are off to find the next magic pill to spark recovery. The trick is to *not* "throw the baby out with the bath water." in this case, you don't have to get rid of incentives. Just be careful in using them that they don't kill the motivation to do good work.
>
> Source: Alfie Kohn, *Punished by Rewards: The Trouble with Gold Stars, Incentive Plans, A's, Praise, and Other Bribes*, (Boston: Houghton Mifflin, 1993).

become an accepted and even expected part of a total compensation package. But the degree to which incentives have dominated some pay programs is problematic. Moreover, the philosophy and intent behind any number of reward systems are suspect. In some instances, they have been used to buy labor "on the cheap," particularly where the base compensation has been reduced to minimal levels. Not only are such programs unconscionable, they're largely ineffective from most any perspective.

Above all else, enlightened managers understand you can't buy motivation. It has to come from within. But managers can impact the context and conditions that enhance people's desire to view work as satisfying and personally fulfilling. And there's no cutting corners to having that kind of impact on employees.

Evidence to the Contrary

Smart managers understand that the subject of incentives is complex. As noted above, some experts maintain that incentives are ineffective for improving long-term performance, particularly if incentives are removed after having been in place for some specified period. They argue that performance actually deteriorates over time; further, incentives not only direct attention away from the inherent satisfaction that comes from work itself toward the stars, prizes, and cash awards of immediate gratification, but also have an adverse impact on motivation. And the experts have data that appear to support their claims.

Others maintain that incentives are vital to increasing productivity and that without them employees would have little or no inclination to improve performance. Indeed, they contend, employees are fundamentally lazy and their motivation comes only from rewards.

Regardless of their persuasion, on one key point experts on both sides of the issue agree: *incentives influence increased performance in the short term.* Consequently, experienced managers understand the need to design and implement new incentives on a continuing basis for repeated short-term gains, whenever there is an incentive component to the total compensation package.

Another principle seems to apply to both schools of thought, namely, that people respond to the influence of incentives out of a sense of *personal choice.* Their choice is most probably determined by a perceived or actual need. Applying Abraham Maslow's theory based on a hierarchy of needs, employees at the lower end of the pay spectrum are generally concerned about satisfying primary needs, e.g., food, shelter, security. As these needs become satisfied, employees are motivated to pursue higher-level needs, such as personal fulfillment, job satisfaction, self-actualization.

The implication for managers is this: if a base compensation program generally meets the needs of employees, pay becomes a "non-issue." It may not be a "satisfier," but at the very least it will not be a "dissatisfier." If pay is sufficient, then, managers are more readily able to direct attention to the nature and quality of the work. As the organization prospers through the collective efforts of its members, fair and equitable distribution of rewards continues to ensure that pay is a non-issue. Moreover, as employees advance according to their hierarchy of needs, their motives may be influenced more readily in the direction of personal and organizational fulfillment.

Experienced managers know that rewards for entry-level employees, i.e., those lower in the pay spectrum, usually need be more cash-based, whereas employees with longer service or

UPS: Employer of Choice

Competing in tight labor markets and vying for workers to do difficult work at peak nighttime hours, United Parcel Service implemented a program targeted at students. Collaborating with state and local officials, the giant carrier offered free tuition, free books, and subsidized housing to qualified applicants. The result after one year was a 90% retention rate, compared with tenures of eight or nine weeks for non-student personnel. In this instance, responding to individual needs resulted in an enormous success for employees, employer, and the community as a whole.

higher in the compensation scheme may be influenced more by cash-equivalent or non-cash rewards, such as earned credits for credit-base benefits programs, education assistance, or extra time off. We'll discuss these reward concepts more fully in Chapter 10.

The challenge for managers lies in finding ways to influence employee and non-employee resources to achieve and stay motivated for the right reasons, not only for the short term but also over the long haul.

Context, Content, and Caring

Laying a good foundation is an important principle in any endeavor; it applies equally to the area of recognizing and rewarding employees. Smart managers begin by paying attention to the basics.

- They create constructive climates or cultures.
- They provide information—both "need to know" and "nice to know."
- They design whole, meaningful jobs.
- They supply needed tools, training, technology, equipment, etc.
- They offer continued guidance and support.

They also recognize that providing recognition and rewards is a little like farming. To produce good yields, you have to begin by preparing the soil. In the business of managing, "preparing the soil" means creating the right culture. To be more specific, think of *culture* as the *context* in which an organization's collective activities occur. The dimensions of any given culture, as we'll discuss in Chapter 5, are varied and largely reflective of the strategies, styles, and behaviors of its leaders and managers. The more aligned a culture is with the mission of the organization and its strategic objectives, the more likely people are to behave in ways that are congruent with the organization's mission, vision, and values. For example, if customer service is a high priority, it generally follows that the way in which people work with one another, treat one another, and regard one another will reflect in the quality of service provided to customers. Conversely, if a culture is critical, hurtful, or perhaps even repressive, customer service will suffer.

By extension, the culture of any organization reflects in its reward and recognition systems and the ways in which managers relate to their people. If your culture values people and if everything you say and do as a manager is congruent with your values system, employees will respond appropriately. Recognition will be seen as an ongoing process for expressing appreciation and for affirming the constructive efforts of your employees. Similarly, you must tailor rewards to the needs of your employees—individually and collectively. Think of rewards as a natural extension of your recognition and compensation systems. The intent behind your programs must be to be *fair*," i.e., appropriate recompense for appropriate contributions.

Alternatively, if the culture of an organization does not value its members, even though the official rhetoric may say otherwise, recognition by its leaders and managers will be viewed with skepticism and rewards will be deemed as something "owed."

Job *content* plays an important part in how people feel about their work and how motivated they are to produce. Too often employees are made to conform to structure, including poorly designed jobs, when, in fact, it ought to be the other way around. Structure should be changed to support people. Witness the massive movement in the United States to teach employees in team-based environments how to redesign their jobs or reengineer work processes. Encouraging employees to improve the design and content of their jobs is not only a great form of recognition, it's also good business!

> ### Check Your Intentions
>
> Smart managers understand that the adage "what goes around comes around" readily applies to recognition and reward systems. To ensure maximum effectiveness, such systems must be "employee-centered," i.e., designed and implemented with the employee in mind. If the intent behind your initiatives is "right-spirited," employees will recognize that and treat them in the same spirit. If you're at all devious or manipulative, expect the worst. It won't be long before employees will spot your ulterior motives. If you understand that your responsibility and goals revolve around helping employees and the organization get better and better at serving customers, you'll hardly ever go wrong.

Work with your employees to determine how you can best provide support. Begin by *caring* about what they care about. Listen to their wants, concerns, ideas, and dreams. Listening is a meaningful form of recognition. Being responsive is even better.

Also, understand that information is the lifeblood of any organization. Keeping employees informed means taking an open-book approach, so they can become more knowledgeable about the economics and dynamics of your business, industry, and marketplace. So, again, "what goes around comes around." The more you care about your people and what will make them successful, the more they'll care about you and your organization.

Putting the Accent on the Right Syl-lá-ble!

Too often managers make the mistake of focusing on the wrong parts of an equation, the wrong elements of a business process, the wrong button that, supposedly, will motivate people to do this or that. Any number of managers have found, for example, that focusing on errors—whether they be personal errors, production errors, or team errors—produces more errors! When managers have instead emphasized continuous improvement, product quality, and individual and team learning, errors have dropped to nearly nothing.

Relying solely on monetary rewards, incentive gimmicks, prizes, contests, and so on is placing emphasis on the wrong syl-lá-ble. If you don't address the underlying fundamentals for improved performance, such as job design, information sharing, needed resources, and supervisory support—all of which are forms of recognition—you run the risk of wasting resources, time, money, and opportunity!

Analyze each situation to determine if it is a "reward" problem or something else. If you determine rewards are appropriate, then consider the persons for whom the rewards are intended. Remember: new job entrants at the lower end of the pay spectrum are generally looking for cash opportunities. Here again, you can't assume. You must ask. There was a time when people at the lower end of the pay scale were supplemental wage earners, such as "empty nesters" who were looking for fun and enjoyment in a workplace setting. If, on the other hand, you have a recent graduate who loves technology, the reward may be new equipment or software. In other words, tailor the reward to meet the needs of the individual employee "customer" and you'll most assuredly meet the needs of the ultimate customer, with a capital "C."

But, above all, construct work assignments and challenges that will capture the interests and motivation of those assigned to do the work. Place your emphasis on "work as its own reward" by designing work that is inherently rewarding!

Consider the case of the professional sales team whose boss announced a new program of incentives, with a point system for every task associated with prospecting, qualifying, selling, and servicing customers: so many calls in a day would earn so

---

Opportunity's Calling!

CAUTION!

The managers of a direct marketing organization, concerned with the need to increase sales, directed operators to limit their time with customers to three minutes. "Take more orders faster and sales will rise" was the assumption. Operator performance was monitored with an elaborate tracking and productivity system, but the increases didn't come. It wasn't until a consultant—with input from employees—recommended "prolonging the customer experience" and "increasing the *size of each* order" that sales began to rise. The change was so successful, the company had to hire more operators to write even more business. The point: by letting employees do the right stuff the right way, they feel better about their work—an incentive in itself that can result in better performance.

many points, the sale of specific items would result in so many more points, and so on. To ensure successful implementation of the program, a consultant was introduced, whose principal responsibility was to educate staff on the intricacies of the new system. When members of the *top* sales team asked how their sales performance would be evaluated under the new system and how they were to be compensated, they were told to forget what they'd learned and concentrate on "points." When they tried to explain how they were approaching the market and servicing their clients, they were told they didn't understand selling. It wasn't long before morale began to deteriorate and the top performers started looking for positions outside the company. Fortunately, management eventually canned the program and sales performance improved.

So, put the emphasis on the right syl-lá-ble, and you and your employees will stay well ahead of the pack.

Rewarding as a Matter of Choice

The old paradigm of "climbing the organization ladder" to get ahead is virtually a model of the past. With flatter organizations and more integrated processes, "horizontal advancement" is the new paradigm. It used to be a manager could recognize the accomplishments of an employee with a promotion or adjust a salary by increasing responsibility, but not any more. Today's environment emphasizes broader job assignments, multitasking, integrated activities, i.e., doing more with less. The only way to "get ahead" is to grow horizontally, by acquiring more knowledge, more skills, more experiences. In brief, it's the world of the free agent, where value is currency and interesting work means increased market worth.

Smart managers know how to recognize the internal drivers, the motivators, the hot buttons within each and every person for whom they are responsible. Their secret tool is *choice*. They know that if they provide options, choices, and alternatives, employees will respond positively in attitude and performance. Providing choices and recognizing desires is one powerful formula for the people-savvy manager.

Horizontal advancement underscores the importance of recognition. It signals, "You're growing and you're valued." By focusing on employees, their work, and work assignments and by engaging in enlightened practices in all areas of responsibility—especially in matters of recognition and reward—smart managers are shifting attention to the creative process of work as its own reward. They're establishing new priorities, knowing they will realize maximum returns for their creativity in designing *opportunities* for their employees—the free agents of a new workplace.

In Chapter 8 we'll discuss how successful managers use the element of "choice" to recognize and reward employees and partners outside the organization alike.

Manager's Checklist for Chapter 2

❑ Quid pro quo incentives have been largely used to manipulate human behavior and have done little to focus employee attentions on work as its own reward. Moreover, evidence seems to suggest incentives have an adverse impact on long-term performance in general.

❑ Motivation is something that exists within people. Managers cannot mandate that others be motivated, but they can influence others to become motivated by offering choices, opportunities, and respect.

❑ Money, in and of itself, cannot motivate others unless they are already inclined, but it can be a "satisfier" or a "dissatisfier" depending on whether it's too much or too little. In an ideal world, managers need to make money a "nonissue" so employees can focus on the job to be done.

❑ In the workplace of the future, one of the most powerful rewards will be the reward of *choice*.

The Human Nature of Work

There's a story about a traveler who was unable to speak the language of the people whose country he was passing through. In an attempt to communicate his needs, he began speaking very slowly in the language of his country of origin. Being unable to elicit the desired response, he continued to speak even more slowly, while increasing the volume of his voice. Soon he began gesturing and shouting at the top of his lungs, one word at a time—very, *very* slowly. Of course, he was no more effective in his extreme state of agitation than he was when he began.

Certainly, a rational person would understand that to communicate effectively you need to speak the language of the person you're addressing. And yet, managers make this mistake every day, assuming others will understand perfectly, just because they're of the same species or from the same organization, community, country, or planet.

People are different! One author has capitalized on that fact by noting the difference in communication styles between people according to gender: "men are from Mars and women are from Venus." But differences go further. No two individuals have matching fingerprints or matching voice patterns or identical appearances; even identical twins have distinguishing features and characteristics that differentiate one from the other. Savvy managers know that to communicate effectively they need to speak in a language that is intelligible to each and every individual. Moreover, savvy managers understand that communication is a "whole person" experience—for both parties.

Effective communication begins with listening and continues through speaking, touching, hearing, and seeing. Communication is the primary means—and a very powerful one—by which managers *recognize* employees.

Roadblocks to positive and productive communication arise when managers become too bossy or too opinionated, when they use fear and intimidation to threaten others, or when they demean or belittle. There will be understanding in such situations between manager and employees, but the results are likely to be resentment, distrust, and a reduced desire to perform well.

> ### Communication Involves the Whole Person
> **Smart Managing**
>
> Ever wonder why words alone don't always convey the message? Smart managers know that actions and a bunch of other stuff speak louder than words. Here's the breakdown of the components of communication:
>
> | Dimension | Percent |
> | --- | --- |
> | Words | 7% |
> | Facial Expression | 23% |
> | Tone of Voice | 20% |
> | Body Language | 50% |
>
> Source: Instructional Fair, Inc., Grand Rapids, MI, 1994.

The failure to express feelings or to express them appropriately creates distrust and causes misunderstandings. Feelings, expressed constructively, convey authenticity on the part of the manager and facilitate. The expression of feelings reduces differences and builds trust.

Recognizing employees requires you to listen to their needs, wants, ideas, opinions, and even dreams. And, just like a traveler in a foreign land, you need to speak the "language" of the person with whom you wish to communicate. The more versed you become in the "customs" and "traditions" that frame his or her perspective and the more respectful you are of the employee's special talents, the better you will become at communicating. As a manager, you will be paying the highest compliment to the other person by recognizing his or her individual uniqueness. Also, employees will be more inclined to want to return the compliment by taking the time to communicate in your "language" to better understand your ideas, your opinions, your wants, and your needs.

Of course, communication, i.e., recognition, takes time. All too often, managers will try taking shortcuts by throwing money at what they perceive to be the problem rather than taking *time* to communicate and influence through increased understanding and mutual respect.

Interpersonal Relationships

To understand the importance of recognition, we must appreciate that we as human beings need both to receive and to give affirmation, i.e., acceptance and respect. This idea of affirmation can turn people off. But wise managers recognize that affirmation is nourishment for the "soul" of individuals and organizations alike; without it, our emotional development and well-being are compromised.

In organizational communities affirmation, affection, and respect are expressed in various forms of recognition, including rewards. As a manager you must appreciate and act in ways that affirm your employees, if you are to enhance their well-being and overall performance. After all, helping employees succeed is an important part of your responsibility.

Various experts espouse the "tough boss" theory on the premise that

Feelings First
A senior executive for a Japanese-owned financial services organization remarked how impressed she was with the Japanese style of managing in her organization. "They ask first, 'How do you feel about (a situation)?' Then, 'What do you think about it?' And finally, 'What do you want to do?'" *Feel, think, act*—the sequence is designed to recognize the individual first by honoring feelings.

The Eyes Have It

TRICKS OF THE TRADE

Two teams of young volleyball players were divided according to "dark" eyes and "blue" eyes. At the start of the game, coaches of the dark-eyed team stressed how superior dark-eyed athletics were. Soon the dark-eyed team led the scoring. At the end of the period, coaches for the opposite side produced contradictory "evidence" that blue-eyed players were superior. As the game continued, the blue-eyed players pulled ahead. At the conclusion, coaches for both sides declared their assertions were bogus. Personal encouragement and self-perception were the keys. The players learned all "eyes" have potential to succeed.

---

employees respond with increased productivity and performance beyond their self-imposed limits if the manager is a taskmaster and commands the respect of employees. While that may indeed be the case up to a point, the preponderance of evidence suggests that creativity, productivity, and personal fulfillment are far greater over a longer period of time in situations involving more humanistic and encouraging leadership. Employees feel motivated out of a sense of a supportive relationship with their manager and the shared belief they can make a difference.

All managers agree that time is a precious commodity. "Time is money," as the saying goes. But, when it comes to leadership and effective interpersonal relationships, this is especially true. There's another saying managers need to appreciate: we spend time with things (and people) we love. Managing people is one of the most important responsibilities managers have. And it's one of the most powerful ways in which managers can recognize people. Time spent working with and leading others is an investment, and when it comes to recognizing employees, there are no shortcuts!

Boundaries

In today's environment, managers must appreciate the significance of both personal and organizational boundaries. Personal boundaries relate to matters of mutual respect and the appreciation of diverse talents and contributions, as we will discuss further in this chapter. Knowing the nature and extent of personal boundaries enables managers to *personalize* their approach to recognizing and rewarding employees.

But the savvy manager knows that personal boundaries can change from day to day, even moment to moment. So too with organizational boundaries. Organizational boundaries as we have known them are changing. And the nature of this change is having a profound effect on the way managers must recognize and reward employees as a group.

The traditional organization structure of boxes and lines, bosses and subordinates, functions and finite jobs contributed to a system of individual workers, where each employee was, in effect, working for the organization almost independently of other employees, even those doing the same job. Consequently, every employee's job was designed, valued, and compensated on the basis of seeming individual contribution. The net effect was to ensure that individuals cared less about the organization as a whole and more about themselves—what they earned, how much of a raise they got, where they fell on the salary scale. Today's organizations are moving away from the traditional structures of boxes and lines, where there were boundaries formed by level, position, function, and restrictive policies and procedures, to structures that are more flexible, more fluid, even "boundaryless."

Replacing the old boundaries of boxes and lines, department names, and job titles are new boundaries:*

> **Key Term**
>
> **"Boundaryless" organization** An organization that makes all of the barriers—vertical, horizontal, external, and geographic—much more permeable, allowing information, ideas, resources, and energy to flow throughout the organization and with business partners.
>
> The term "boundaryless" was coined by General Electric CEO Jack Welch in the company's 1990 annual report to signify a vision erasing the barriers dividing the organization from its key constituencies outside of GE and its employees from one another within. He wanted to erase the distinctions between domestic and foreign operations and the "labels"—such as "management," "salaried," and "hourly"—to get people working together.

*Larry Hirschhorn and Thomas Gilmore, "The New Boundaries of the 'Boundaryless' Company," *Harvard Business Review*, May-June 1992, p. 107.

> ## Rewarding Cooperation
> One multinational corporation recognizes "cross-organizational cooperation" in its annual award program for business unit heads. Even though each unit manager is rewarded on the basis of his or her business results, corporate success overall is dependent upon the full cooperation of all. For example, rather than holding excess inventory to protect business results in one country, a unit head must share in the event of a shortage at a unit in another country. Because of the policy of compensating for cooperation as well as unit performance, unit chiefs and the corporation stand to win in the high-stakes game of global competition.

- *Authority*: "Who's in charge of what?" Leaders must remain open to criticism and followers must be able to challenge superiors.
- *Task*: "Who does what?" People must depend on others they don't control and specialists must understand the jobs of others.
- *Political*: "What's in it for us?" Every employee must defend his or her own interests while supporting the interests of the organization. Win-win becomes more important than win-lose.
- *Identity*: "Who is and isn't 'us'?" People must feel pride without devaluing others and remain committed without undermining outsiders.

Managers must understand the significance of these new boundaries and the benefits of new organizational structures over the traditional structures. To recognize and reward individuals and groups based on the old boundaries ensures rigidity, self-centered thinking and behavior, and limited success. Recognizing and rewarding people in the "boundaryless" way requires complete understanding, managerial skill, and relentless innovation to ensure maximum flexibility, enlightened self-interest ("everyone must win"), and greatest benefits for all.

Mutual Respect

Understanding and respecting personal boundaries is the highest form of recognition in any relationship, be it personal, social, or professional. And the complexity of our American society is making the area of personal boundaries even more significant.

Creating an environment that is *safe* and *respectful* of personal boundaries is not only important, but in some instances also required by law. For example, it is unlawful to harass others in the workplace based on gender, age, race, religion, national origin, handicap, etc. And that requirement applies not only to interactions between managers and employees, but also to interactions between employees and managers, between employees and other employees, even between outside personnel, such as vendors and relatives, and employees. Responsible managers know and enforce laws that protect employees—but they also know that

> **Key Term**
>
> **Personal Boundaries**
> The *physical, social,* and *psychological* "space" that helps define the extent of one's *self. Physical* space generally extends all around a person to about the length of an outstretched arm. If someone comes within that space, an individual may feel crowded, even violated, depending on the circumstances. If others are joking about people of a particular race or nationality, one may be offended based on *social* identification with those being derided. Similarly, demeaning or disrespectful behavior is a violation of *psychological* boundaries because of the adverse impact on one's sense of self-worth.

bringing out the best in others requires measures beyond those specified by state, local, and federal regulations.

Respect is the bedrock of recognition. Without it, no amount of manipulation, cajoling, explanation, or outright dissembling will compensate for its absence. Meeting personal and group needs, discussing expectations, honoring the privacy of others, listening attentively and actively, expressing appreciation, and showing kindness and caring are all ways of exemplifying respect.

That's not to say that, even if you do everything perfectly as a manager, you won't offend someone. How people perceive behavior is mostly quite personal. An innocent remark or the omission of some form of acknowledgment may be perceived as a slight. Once aware of any offense, caring managers are quick to recover and right the perceived wrong.

Signs of Disrespect

Actions that inhibit constructive recognition include:

Intimidation	Derision
Unwanted touching	Offensive joking
Taunting	Teasing
Sexual come-ons	Ordering/demanding
Calling names	Reading personal information
Invading personal space	Gossiping/backbiting
Gesturing	Publicizing personal confidences
Belittling	Interrupting/ "over-talking"
Threatening	Physical bullying

Adapted from *Violence Intervention and Prevention*, Minneapolis: Johnson Institute, 1994.

Ask any employee what he or she would most appreciate on a daily basis and nine times out of ten you'll hear, "I'd like people to say 'please' and 'thank you.'" Simple, isn't it? But, in our hurry-up world of doing more with less, it's the most forgotten form of recognition and respect—and the most wanted.

Embracing Diversity

Mention the phrase "embracing diversity" and most managers think of the need to accept and appreciate people of diverse racial and national origins. And while that certainly is part of it, an even broader interpretation includes people with differing opinions and ideas. In a world of ever-expanding opportunity and multinational considerations, managers need to appreciate now more than ever the preferences, perspectives, and talents of their people who come from all walks of life—especially because they match the profiles of the customers being served. Indeed, they *are* customers in the world at large, as well as employees. The benefit of realizing this lies in the freedom it gives managers to appreciate that employees have much to offer in the way of ideas and business contributions.

Imagine how different the world might be had some manager at 3M resisted the idea, i.e., the "mistake," of a pad of paper with too much glue between the pages? We might never have seen Post-its®, those little sticky papers that come in all shapes, sizes, and colors and that have even become easel

Have the 'LAST' Word

Even the best of managers may be perceived as having violated personal boundaries or engaged in offensive behavior. When that happens, the best course of action is to:

(L) Listen attentively without being defensive.

(A) Acknowledge the other person's feelings.

(S) Specify what you'll do to ensure it doesn't happen again.

(T) Thank the person for expressing his or her concerns.

Responding in this way recognizes the person's concerns, expresses respect for his or her personal needs, and allows both parties to move forward.

sheets and rolls of paper that can be unfurled to chart the flow of new ideas in workshops and schools around the world. Or what if some manager at Procter & Gamble had resisted the idea, i.e., another "mistake," of a bar of soap with too much air? We might never have seen Ivory soap, the bar that's so pure it floats. With both examples, it took managers who were not threatened by something different and who were encouraging of employees with innovative ideas and discoveries.

Unfortunately, companies are losing many new ideas and innovative ways as employees who are inhibited by traditional views and the resistance to diverse approaches leave—sometimes to form their own companies. Enlightened managers respect diversity of experience, perspective, and thinking and encourage it through teamwork. It's not just a good idea; it's an opportunity to improve and innovate.

If employees don't feel accepted and appreciated for their differences, they won't be motivated to contribute to their potential. Some part of their identity will remain private, some special energy with be held in reserve, some unique gift will not be shared, and the workplace and the world will be that much less enriched.

Leadership and Recognition

A study reported in 1993* that the characteristic most admired in leaders was that they be *honest.* Other characteristics included

*James M. Kouzes, Barry Z. Posner, and Tom Peters, *Credibility: How Leaders Gain and Lose It, Why People Demand It* (San Francisco: Jossey-Bass Publishers, 1993).

forward-looking, inspiring, competent, fair-minded, supportive, broadminded, intelligent, straightforward, and *courageous.* Words that best described the feelings of those working with leaders they trusted were *valued, motivated, enthusiastic, challenged, inspired, capable, supported, powerful,* and *respected.* Savvy managers know, as this study indicates, that recognizing employees as valued resources and rewarding them with challenging opportunities is one of the best way to influence motivation in others.

Appreciating Differences

A range of tools are available to help managers and employees appreciate the value of different thinking and behavioral styles. Here are some representative instruments:

- *Myers-Briggs Temperament Indicator (MBTI)*
- Human Synergistics' *Life Styles Inventory (LSI) I and II*
- Stuart Atkins' *LIFO (Life Orientations) Training*

For best results, engage the services of a certified trainer and facilitator. These instruments, when properly administered and utilized, are particularly useful for building skills in teamwork.

If you've ever been on an Outward Bound experience or some executive retreat involving outdoor exercises, then you've undoubtedly experienced or at least know about exercises that require a participant—usually a boss—to exhibit trust in others by falling backwards while blindfolded into the arms of waiting team members or by allowing them to convey the "wounded" leader over some dangerous terrain. The purpose of the drill is to foster a sense of trust, confidence, and teamwork in all participants. It is precisely that sense of trust that leaders need to exhibit toward employees. It's the highest form of recognition and extremely effective in inspiring commitment.

In many organizations the mere mention of union organizing sends shivers down the spine of even the most unflappable CEO. Among a host of concerns are the possibility of adversarial relationships between union leadership and management, periodic unrest among employees over workplace grievances, work stoppages and lockouts, disruptions of business operations and customer relations, and the mandate to bargain on a

> ### Entrusting the Future
>
> The CEO of a small manufacturing firm known around the world for its quality products and processes proudly pointed to the mechanical assembly line—outfitted with little levers and other mechanisms—designed and operated by employees. "It was their idea. The product produced by their line now contributes more than half our bottom-line profits," he reported. "Their innovation resulted in our idling a computerized robotics system, it turned out, we didn't need. If you hire good people, train 'em right, and treat 'em right, you just have to trust their instincts to do the right thing."

broad range of issues including wages, benefits, and working conditions. In the face of an organizing drive, management's first reaction is to circle the wagons and attempt to convince employees that they do not need union representation.

Perhaps the most striking example of trust is exhibited by the leadership of the Toyota Motor Manufacturing Georgetown, KY plant. Employee involvement is a way of life at TMM. Organized in teams, employees are empowered to shut down entire assembly line operations if they detect a problem in the manufacturing process. Leadership trusts employee judgment, recognizes competence, and rewards team members with the power to act independently. But trust doesn't stop there. Asked about union representation, leadership responds differently from management in most other organizations. "It's up to the team. We trust their judgment. If they believe they need union representation, we respect their decision." Since the opening of the plant in the early 1990s, there has been no union representation.

Control and Influence

Mention the word "control" and the first thing most people picture is some kind of "theory X" style boss, whose *modus operandi* is pulling the strings of employees to see how far they can be pushed and how high they can jump. This concept leaves little freedom for individual initiative and on-the-job discretion, and it certainly doesn't recognize people's abilities and potential for meaningful contributions.

> ### Checking In
>
> Recognizing employees through collaborative work processes is much like facilitating a meeting:
> - Make sure everyone is mentally "checking in."
> - Be certain employees know the objectives and are committed to working to achieve desired outcomes.
> - Train everybody in the principles of consensus building and joint decision making.
> - Stress the importance of participation. Everybody has something to contribute to the team.
> - Don't dominate the process or allow others to. Be a facilitator.
> - Ask for constructive feedback, input, ideas.
> - Trust the process. Well-intentioned people with an understanding of goals and sound methods will work toward productive ends.
> - Continually ask for concerns, criticisms, suggestions, opinions, and ideas.

At the other extreme is the "abandoning" boss who hates managing people and prefers to be left to do her or his own thing. Often, this type of manager either focuses more on being an individual contributor than manager or allows his or her personal agenda for getting ahead or desire to hobnob with the "movers and shakers" to take precedence over managing people.

Both types of manager choose not to recognize their employees, but for different reasons. Theory X managers perceive employees as objects with little or no redeeming value. Negligent managers perceive them as annoyances or distractions that, if left unencouraged and unnoticed, will—with any luck—go away or become virtually invisible.

Both are extreme models of control, opposites but similar to the extent that each fails to recognize employees and value their full potential. Somewhere in between these two extremes lies a third model of control that is more collaborative and empowering. This model not only recognizes the capabilities of employees, but also incorporates employees into a system of mutual accountability and responsibility. Of the three, this is the most effective form of control, in that it neither overcontrols nor abandons employees; indeed, it demands the best employees have to offer by creating structures, processes, opportunities, and expectations for individual and group contributions. In other words, it is a model of *influence*.

The old saw, "You catch more flies with honey than with vinegar," certainly applies when it comes to managing, controlling, and influencing others. We'll discuss this further in Chapter 4.

Self-Esteem

Building self-esteem is almost an art. Successful managers know the importance of both individual and organizational self-esteem. Recognizing employees in constructive, meaningful ways contributes to better performance and greater company pride. In a world where upward mobility and recognition through advancement are limited, the new paradigm for professional growth is *personal development. Continuous learning*—whether it's new skills, new systems, or new regulations—and *building self-confidence* are two key factors in personal development. Employees committed to personal development are more likely to withstand the forces of economic downturns and cutbacks.

> **Key Term**
>
> **Self-esteem** How a person regards him- or herself. Positive or high self-esteem means that individuals have self-respect and feel good about themselves and their abilities. This translates into respect for others and the desire to work with others to achieve shared goals. Employees with positive self-esteem are better employees and are usually better equipped to help the organization achieve its objectives.

Equally important, managers who encourage and support personal development are better able to help their employees cultivate what they need most in a competitive global environment—a healthy sense of self-worth.

Managers who see the good in others and who exhibit "can do" attitudes have a positive influence on their employees. Positive attitudes and positive self-impressions are contagious. When people feel good about themselves, work appears meaningful and there's energy and motivation to do more. New ideas are generated. People are inclined to try new things and even

Do unto Others

The collections manager for a national retailer, whose department was a benchmark for the industry, had a special knack for building self-esteem. "I always surprise people by being friendly but firm," he explained. "I treat them the way I'd want to be treated if I had outstanding debt." Employees loved him because he cared about them and customers respected him for the way he allowed them to retain their dignity. And he worked to preserve his own self-esteem. "It's how I feel about myself at the end of the day that's important. That's what I care most about."

take moderate risks. Problems are seen as challenges. And, more important, people are more willing to work together in pursuit of shared objectives.

In contrast, when employees are not properly recognized and respected, they tend to protect their self-esteem. They pull back, they avoid taking chances by making suggestions or offering ideas, and they do only what is required, in the interest of personal security and survival.

Successful managers know that to get the best results they must recognize employees in ways that build self-esteem. They compliment. They encourage in writing and in person. They celebrate accomplishments—and even constructive attempts. They look for every opportunity to reinforce personal pride. This approach certainly demands practice, patience, and persistence; but for "can do" managers the alternative, dispirited employees with avoidance tendencies, is unthinkable!

Organizational Pride

Managers understand the value of organizational pride. When people feel good about what they are accomplishing as individuals and as a group, they're motivated to do more. Whether it's increasing productivity, improving quality, reducing errors, or reaching for the stars, organizational pride is exhilarating—and it makes for good business.

Pride in one's organization does not come as a result of mere rhetoric and it does not come overnight. It begins with an expectation and continues with the celebration of one "heroic" deed at a time. Vigilant managers are constantly on the lookout for individual accomplishments that are consistent with desired results.

And they celebrate those accomplishments. Here are some of the ways:

- Compliment and express appreciation in person.
- Acknowledge accomplishments in meetings with fellow employees.
- Throw parties, the size depending on the importance of the accomplishment.
- Communicate the good news to higher-ups.
- Write articles in internal publications—with pictures.
- Take out an ad to celebrate publicly.
- Ask the "hero" or "heroine" to teach others the secrets of their success.
- Present certificates or other commemorative symbols.
- Provide some expression of appreciation in the form of financial or in-kind gift.
- Include a picture and story in annual reports to stockholders.

The list could go on and on. But most important, seize the moment to recognize and appreciate employees.

To recognize employees on an ongoing basis, some organizations build entire customer communication programs around

People Make the Difference

When the young executive left "big banking" and moved to a start-up operation, former colleagues doubted the wisdom of his decision. Valuing personalized service, he began touting the outstanding customer service at the new bank. Complimentary letters from customers first trickled in, then poured in, as staff delivered even more notable service. In addition to recognizing them within the company, he bought ads spotlighting individual employees. Within a short time the bank's reputation for personalized service eclipsed competitors'. Now CEO, he leads this growing regional bank with a recognized reputation for service above and beyond the call of duty.

the accomplishments and outstanding service of their employees. Organizations like Federal Express and others, as we'll see
in Chapter 9, "immortalize" employee achievements like some
sort of folklore or revered annals for emulation by other
employees in the future. To be certain, such programs enhance
the reputation of the organization, but the purpose of such initiatives is to appreciate and recognize employees.

Vision, Mission, Values, and Other Dreams

Dreamers, visionaries, and other change agents know that to
make a difference in the world they need to hook the dreams of
others to a compelling vision for the future. Martin Luther King,
Gandhi, Mother Teresa, and John F. Kennedy are examples of
people with vision. And each found people throughout their life
journeys whose deeds could be celebrated and acclaimed as
representative of the greater dream.

Various organizations have formulated visions and missions,
usually as part of a strategic planning process, to capture the
hearts, minds, and commitment of others, particularly employees. But perhaps the most powerful means of recognizing the
importance of people has come in the form of values statements and guiding principles.

To encourage others to do the "right thing," organizational
leaders have crafted such systems to recognize the basic good
in others and to appeal to people of character and good intentions to answer some higher calling, some lofty purpose. Such
systems are almost inspirational in their ability to enliven the
soul and spirit of employees, to connect with their personal
identity and their basic need for inner sustenance. Insightful
managers know instinctively that they must recognize the soul
and the spirit as well as the other components of their employees, if they are to be totally effective in their role as managers.

To accomplish this aspect of recognizing employees, as a
manager you need to stand for something, e.g., "commitment,"
"achievement," "going the extra mile." And you need to develop
values or guiding principles for your department or area of
responsibility that represent the identity that you want for your-

---

For Example

The "Golden" Principle

The CEO of a large manufacturing firm determined he would introduce *kaizen* (Japanese for the process of continuous improvement) to his employees and adopt a set of principles that would guide employees throughout the company in working with one another. While some of the principles were subject to interpretation, one was absolutely inviolate, that of "building self-esteem." So sacred was the principle that two years into the initiative the firm let go three top executives. "They knew how to get results in the old-style way—by humiliating and intimidating employees," the CEO explained, "but they refused to recognize our employees as valued human beings."

---

self and your employees. Examples of such principles might be:

- Treat one another with dignity and respect
- Value every customer as special
- Build products that satisfy needs and exceed expectations
- Act in socially responsible ways

To be sure, your system of values needs to be congruent with the objectives and values of your organization, but it also can and must be customized to your area of responsibility. And if you develop it in cooperation with your employees, you will have begun the recognition process properly.

When Systems Support People

Traditional organization structures represent hierarchical systems in which standards are determined centrally and control rests comfortably in the hands of a few. How an organization is structured depends largely on what management perceives as the best way to arrange geographically. In such systems, people end up supporting structures rather than the structures supporting people. In such circumstances, the offices of vice presidents, for example, might be located near one another rather than in the departments for which they are responsible.

Given the opportunity to redesign an organization according to how it really works, employees will usually opt for the most functional design—the one that most easily facilitates getting the work done. Most large-systems change efforts that involved employees in the redesign process have resulted in significant improvements in productivity and profitability and increased employee satisfaction. Moreover, by involving employees in the process of redesign, managers are effectively acknowledging the ability of their employees to make good business decisions as well as gaining their commitment to the new structures.

Maybe you're thinking, "That's fine, but my organization is not planning on changing its structure" or "OK, but I don't have the authority to do any large-scale restructuring." So how does this section of the chapter apply to you?

As the popular slogan advises, "Think globally, act locally." Consider what authority you have as a manager to make changes within your area of responsibility.

> ### Managers as Resources
>
> A large manufacturer dedicated to the concept of team-based organization designs situates managers' "offices" on the floor of its plants—right in the middle of all the manufacturing activity. The belief is that managers are there to support the needs of their people. The physical location of their workstations recognizes that need. Asked how he liked it, one manager replied, "At first it felt as if I'd been demoted ....You know, no corner office with a window. But, truthfully, it was the right thing to do. Most of my time is spent with my people."

Newer organization designs are being developed on the basis of logical work flows and the need for human interaction based on job function. Are there any ways to make work flow in your area more logical? Teams and team-based organization designs recognize the value of employees. Consequently, the resources and support they require are built into the structure for their convenience rather than, for example, the convenience of the warehouse. How can you better organize the resources and support for your group of employees and any teams within that group?

Don't answer those questions specifically. Leave the answers to your employees: that's another way of recognizing them. By training, supporting, and empowering employees to make improvements continuously, managers are providing two of the

> **CAUTION!**
>
> ### Excuse Me
>
> If employees are constantly at your door saying, "Excuse me," there's something wrong. If employees look to you for solutions to their problems, there must be something wrong. If you're leaving at the end of the day thoroughly exhausted from putting out too many fires, something's drastically wrong. Examine how you structure decision making. Look at how people are organized and trained to solve problems. Be rigorously honest about your management style. It may be that the structure is serving your need to feel important rather than the important needs of your employees.

most significant forms of recognition—trust and the freedom to influence the future.

Work systems that support people are respectful, purposeful, and powerfully effective. If your employees are not as productive as you'd like, take note of any and all structural obstacles. Consider the following examples of such obstacles:

- The organization design itself
- Policies and procedures
- Communications
- Pay systems
- Value system
- Physical layout
- Tools and equipment
- Materials and supplies

Remember: recognizing employees is a "whole person experience." It's also a "total environment" experience, since nothing happens in a vacuum. It is a powerful form of of individual and group recognition when you take into account the psychological as well as the environmental needs of employees, and address those in a proactive manner.

Manager's Checklist for Chapter 3

❑ Communication is the cornerstone for recognizing employees. Managers must learn the art of communicating with others in their "language," both to understand better and to be understood.

❑ Recognizing employees in the right way requires managers to be aware and respectful of personal boundaries. They also need to understand the nature and extent of the new organizational boundaries—those of authority, task, politics, and personal identity.

❑ Mutual respect will be an important form of recognition in the new workplace. Without it, managers run the risk of experiencing the worst of what "combative cultures" have to offer.

❑ Smart managers will understand the difference between controlling and influencing, particularly in the context of building relationships and increasing trust.

❑ Self-esteem—both personal and organizational—is the desired outcome of an organizational system that recognizes human potential and allows others to experience the joy of achievement and self-actualization.

4

Rewarding Employees by Leading Well

F rustrated over lagging sales and angry with the commissioned force for not producing at the level of projected
sales, the corporate vice president requested that the unit manager have all his sales employees report for an early morning
meeting before the start of business.

As the employees entered the meeting area, a staff assistant
pinned a colored ribbon around the arm of each salesperson—
red, yellow, or blue. Each looked quizzically at the ribbons and
then quietly took a seat. After introducing the vice president, the
unit manager yielded the floor. The VP began by presenting a
chart of the planned sales for the unit. He then went on to discuss the commission plan, illustrating the impressive income
potential that the salespeople could attain at successive levels
of sales productivity. Continuing, he presented information on
the disappointing performance of the unit since its launching a
few months earlier, and he carefully compared the productivity
of the sales associates with that of their counterparts in other
units. Following a brief question-and-answer period, he focused
their attention on the armbands.

"You're probably wondering why you're wearing armbands—and what the significance of the different colors might be," he said. "'Blue' signifies the top performers of this unit. You are achieving sales expectations and have every opportunity to realize the kind of income you and we envision for you."

With that, people began to move about nervously in their seats to see who was wearing which color.

"Those of you who are wearing yellow bands better start paying a lot of attention to those with blue bands, because you need to improve quickly to stay out of trouble. Find out what they're doing to be so successful, emulate their example, and you'll be a lot better off. And finally, you who are wearing red bands better start watching and learning from the 'yellows' and the 'blues' or you won't be here the next time I come to your unit, next month."

With that the meeting concluded in silence. As the salespeople exited the meeting area, they began removing their bands as quickly and as discreetly as possible. In 30 days neither the unit manager nor the corporate vice president saw the increased sales volume they demanded. But, they received a notice from the National Labor Relations Board advising them that the union was seeking to represent the sales staff and had sufficient signatures to seek an election.

As the ranks of "free agents" continue to swell, from both traditional and nontraditional sources, managers are confronted daily with the reality that the world no longer wants or needs "command and control" managers. Moreover, with the rise of the Internet and the widening

> **The Power to Change** **⚠ CAUTION!**
>
> No manager can effectively change someone else. Nor can she or he motivate an employee to do something if the employee is not so inclined. No amount of "carrots" or "sticks" will achieve that end, either. In fact, the only person you, as a manager, can change is yourself.
>
> But, how you change and what you choose to become can have a tremendous influence on others. Indeed, the power of *lasting change* lies in how personally motivated, how passionately compelled employees feel to emulate your example.

Being All One Can Be

"Even the Army's changing," reports retired Army Colonel K. C. Skull. With continued downsizing of the military, recruits are voluntary. "It costs about $50,000 to recruit a soldier and another $50,000 to train 'em. With $100,000 investment 'on the hoof' for a new recruit, especially for one who's volunteered, it takes a different kind of leadership." Asked about his thoughts on managing people, he advised, "Set broad guidelines and delegate everything. You gotta recognize people are there 'cause they want to be and you must reward them with responsibility and accountability."

distances between "free agent" employees and the traditional work setting (with everyone under one roof, so to speak), smart managers are freeing themselves from the illusion of having power and are concentrating instead on the strategies of influence.

The Illusion of Power

Kay Anderson (not her real name) was the administrator for a long-term health care facility for the severely mentally handicapped. Many of the residents had lived at the facility since childhood. The operation was constantly under pressure by the state to reduce costs and manage resources as stringently as possible. Entry-level positions were pegged at minimum wage. Because Kay's facility was state-owned, she had no ability to change pay rates without legislative approval. Morale was low, turnover was high, and resident care was a secondary consideration in the minds of many workers. Almost as a last resort, Kay decided to experiment with a concept she had read about extensively, *self-directed employee teams.*

The experiment began in one area of patient care. Barely had management commissioned the first team when it started another, and then another. Within a year the facility was operating under the new team concept.

Not everything went smoothly and some managers had moments of doubt—but not Kay. She had determined there was no alternative—and turning back was certainly not an option. Gradually, as employees became more and more involved in the concept, attendance began to improve, open job requisitions declined, and even workers' compensation claims were fewer. As team members became more confident in the team process and more competent in their team skills, they began to take on some of the tasks previously handled by managers.

Scheduling—a difficult process in health care, even under normal circumstances—was now being handled by team members, working within established guidelines. In the past, employees might have been reluctant to respond to a supervisor's call to report to work to cover some special situation or an unexpected absence. Now, however, employees were more successful in getting their fellow team members to respond. And, in the year of the "big snowstorm," when other facilities incurred huge overtime expenses in premium pay for staff coverage of the emergency, Kay's was the only one in the state to finish the year on budget—thanks to the self-managing teams who adjusted schedules to offset the excess hours.

"All the time we were managing the traditional way," she reported, "I thought I was in control. It wasn't until we went to the team concept that I realized it was an illusion. I concluded time spent 'managing' could better be spent developing others to take responsibility for their own lives at work and for the clients and people we all care about."

Certainly, Kay would be the first to admit that leadership in the context of today's environment is hard. But the ultimate reward for her efforts came when families of the residents, who could see how care of their loved ones had improved under the team concept, defended the facility against being closed by the state for budgetary reasons. The legislators, after hearing the testimony of the family members and reviewing the medical and financial performance of the facility, revised the close order and voted to continue operations with increased financial support.

As a manager, it's more important that you rely on building the competencies of those on whom you depend—your employees—because, after all, the competence of your employees is a reflection on your competence as a leader. Even when you think you have the power to change someone's behavior or bend someone's will to do what you want, you really don't. Perhaps you'll be seduced to think you're different from other

> **Getting the Results You Want**
> You can get the best results in today's environment, especially with today's "free agents," if you do the following:
> • Set high standards for employees.
> • Train employees in the skills necessary to do the job.
> • Provide independent reporting mechanisms that allow employees to see for themselves how they're doing against the standards.
> • Work with employees who are not achieving.
> • Make the tough decisions to remove from the system employees who don't perform.
> • Concentrate on building the proficiency of the team.
> • Share power in order to achieve better results.

managers. Perhaps an employee or group of employees will lead you to believe you "made them" do something they didn't want to do, but in reality it really was their decision. What smart managers have come to know is that managers who serve their employees have greater influence over behavior than those who try to exert power.

There's a fundamental traditional value in South Africa, *amuntu abuntu aganta*, that's expressed simply in a proverb, "a person is a person because of other people." It suggests that people are defined by their relationships with other people. As a manager, how you are known, what you stand for, and what kind of manager you are are all a function of how you manage and how your employees regard you as a manager.

If managers behave in ways that are seen as controlling, overpowering, or aggressive, employees will be reluctant to follow their lead. If they do, it certainly won't be for long. Even the most passive employee will regard this type of manager as less than worthy of his or her loyalty and will silently wait for the manager to make a mistake or get what's coming to him or her. On the other hand, if a manager recognizes and respects his or her employees as contributing members of a team and supports them in ways that enhance their potential for success, if employees think that their manager has their best interests at heart, they will reward that manager with respect, commitment, and unwavering support. By recognizing employees in constructive ways, this latter type of manager will be recognized in return. Which manager do you think is more "powerful"?

Getting Priorities Straight

Many managers go about figuring out ways to "motivate" employees to do what they want them to do. Smart managers, on the other hand, realize *people are their business* and go about establishing standards, setting goals, planning objectives, training, and monitoring progress against plan. They do this *before* looking at ways to reward employees financially for the right performance and the right reasons.

Putting emphasis on performance is better than focusing on what people earn. But focusing on desired *outcomes* is an even more effective way of getting attention to the right priorities. The notion of "managing by objectives" was certainly an improved concept of management in its day, but the idea of meeting and achieving objectives suggests that once the objectives are achieved the pursuit is over. Managing to *outcomes*, on the other hand, suggests a sort of ongoing condition that must be maintained *ad infinitum*.

For example, "achieving sales of *X*" is an *objective*. It sets a finite goal for employees; once they've achieved that goal, they move on to another. On the other hand, "satisfied customers" is an *outcome* that has no finite goal. It is a state that is ongoing and continuously changing. Similarly, when managers—and the organizational systems they represent—focus attention on incentives or the economic recompense for performance, it distracts attention away from the outcome of satisfied customers. Certainly, pay is important, but when people are paid appropriately, the economics of work become secondary to the mission of the organization and its desired outcomes.

Leadership and Stewardship

Much has been written about the difference between *managing* and *leading*. Some managers may wonder what these concepts have to do with recognizing and rewarding employees. The answer, succinctly expressed, is "everything!"

How managers behave toward employees speaks volumes in terms of influencing their behavior and recognizing them as contributing members of an organizational community. The annals of corporate leadership are replete with heroes and non-heroes who have behaved in ways that have impacted organizational performance significantly. And how they've recognized and rewarded employees has been a key factor in the success—or failure—of the organizations they've led, as we'll discuss below. Indeed, part of effective leadership behavior involves effectively recognizing employee performance.

In the traditional sense, managing has been characterized by such tasks as planning, organizing, directing, and controlling. In the context of a "managed" environment, employees are generally viewed as objects of direction and control and are, of necessity, highly dependent upon the manager for just about everything. Decision making may be delegated to employees, so long as the issues are fairly mundane and the results consistent with a certain prescribed set of standards. Anything falling outside the boundaries set by the manager must be reserved for the manager to review and approve. In this scenario, employees are not recognized for having any real discretionary ability. Consequently, the need for reward is minimal and, in the mind of the traditional manager, it is the manager who must be regarded as the principal client whom employees need to satisfy, even if it is sometimes at the expense of the customer. This is also not the way an effective leader operates.

As management theory continued to evolve in the 1980s and early 1990s, managers were encouraged to become leaders more than managers, putting "enlightened self-interest" above personal agendas. The role of the leader was characterized by tasks of setting direction, coaching, encouraging, and supporting employees. Indeed, the new leader was to be a resource for employees, rather than the other way around. By acting with enlightened self-interest, namely, doing what was in the best interest of customers and employees, the leader would also be serving his or her own interests at the same time. Phrases like "servant-leader" and "service above self" seemed to capture the

> ### Managing the Right Stuff
>
> Don't do what this manager did. Despite a generous commission program and constant training in customer sales and service, Donna's department was not performing well. The reason became apparent one day when her area manager observed Donna taking inventory with her salesperson. As a customer entered the department, the salesperson interrupted her task to wait on the customer. Donna stepped in and directed the employee to continue taking inventory. Unattended and unassisted, the customer left the department, as the manager went about her business and the area manager looked on in amazement.

spirit of the changed perspective around the boss's job. In the context of this new environment, employees were recognized as competent and capable. They were rewarded with increased decision-making, i.e., they were "empowered" to do the right thing. *Inclusion, participative management,* and *cooperation* were the watchwords of this new world.

Today, management pundits are urging managers to regard themselves more as "stewards" entrusted with the care and safekeeping of all valued employees. In the context of this newer model, employees are credited with intelligence, accountability, and motivation. They are not "owned" or controlled by the manager, as if they were some sort of personal property, but rather they are to be regarded as resources of the organization—"on loan," so to speak, to the manager with the notion that somehow employee interests, values, and abilities will be enhanced for some greater good. Working beyond the boundaries of "enlightened self-interest," the manager now is committed to some higher purpose and vision, transcending the mundane, the petty, and focusing instead on the greater good to be served by those committed to building a better world.

In this model, employees are recognized as partners with managers. Beyond cooperation, *collaboration* is the essence of how organizational members are to achieve shared objectives. Employees are to be regarded with dignity and respect, supported by systems—social, operational, technical, and financial—that reinforce the efficacy of their intentions and support their accomplishments. Their reward is inherent in the nature of their work

Key Term

Enlightened self-interest
Big-picture thinking, understanding the dynamics of the system or community and recognizing that because "we're all in this together," we facilitate our own success by facilitating the success of others—and we undermine our success by not supporting others.

and the satisfaction they bring to others.

While models of leadership and stewardship may sound unrealistic to hard-charging managers trying to make a name for themselves in a highly competitive, fiercely demanding, fast-changing world, the fact is those models are the bedrock on which success is built. Indeed, the attributes of these models determine the shape and complexion of the recognition and reward systems themselves and, more important, the outcomes they help bring about.

Enlightened Interests

"What's in it for me?" is a question every manager should be ready to answer for employees, customers, and key stakeholders alike—in every organization. More important, every manager needs to think and *act* in ways that ensure that employees, customers, and stakeholders benefit from managerial action.

Acting in the interest of others is one of the best forms of recognition and reward we have as human beings. Smart managers know they must connect their needs and wants to those of others, if they are to accomplish what must be done.

For example, if you ask employees to take special care in performing a particular service, you must be able to demonstrate that your request is for some ultimate good, e.g., "customer satisfaction"—and then be able to show how customer satisfaction brings satisfaction to the employees when they know that their own reputations and that of the organization are being enhanced by excellent service. It's a way of answering the question "What's in it for me?" and an effective means for getting things done for the right reasons.

In a world of work that is increasingly characterized by plant closings, flexible staffing, downsizing, and the constant churning of workers, managers must shift from the implicit assumptions of

---

Tips for Stewarding

TRICKS OF THE TRADE

- Aim high. No one covets mediocrity.
- Serve with purpose. Establish principles and values that inspire commitment.
- Pick partners, not prisoners. There's no substitute for motivated people.
- Value others. We are all resources for someone or something else.
- Choose freedom: to participate, act, and achieve desired outcomes.
- Be generous—with your time, treasure, and recognition of others.
- Take the longer view. Stewarding pays dividends in ways that are not just financial, but it takes time.
- Innovate. Nothing kills innovation and motivation like overmanaging.
- Have fun and the rewards will follow.

---

employer/employee relationships that demanded *obedience*—to organizations, bosses, and the promise of lifelong employment—to the explicit encouragement of relationships that foster *collaboration*. To do that, enterprising managers are focusing on *enlightened self-interest* as a means to engage employees by helping them focus on outcomes that not only benefit the enterprise as a whole but also benefit them personally. It helps "free agent" employees see the efficacy of their contribution and their learning—no matter what happens to their "job" or their company. Indeed, managers and employees alike must have a view that their life's work is larger than the temporal relationship of a single position, an isolated moment in time, a title, or even a paycheck.

Talk to dedicated teachers or to caregivers in the healthcare industry, and you'll find they're committed not to their low pay but to the students, patients, and/or clients they serve. Service to others who appreciate them is the single most powerful motivation for being in their fields. Intuitive managers recognize the importance of motivation and professional commitment, and they do everything in their power to construct meaningful assignments to challenge employees and satisfy their needs to use and develop their skills and earn the gratitude of their customers.

Malden Mills owner Aaron Feuerstein could have collected the insurance money when fire destroyed his business in Lawrence, Massachusetts in 1995, and then closed the business and walked away. Instead, he kept more than 1,000 jobless

The Power of Enlightened Self-Interest

Managers acting with enlightened self-interest:

• Envision better worlds, whatever they might be.
• Engage others in the pursuit of vision.
• Recognize employees as "customers"—they look to managers to provide a service.
• Put "customer" interests first—"employee customers" and "customer customers."
• Value excellence.
• Recognize the needs of others and work on their behalf.
• Appreciate the dignity of work as an expression of the creative process.
• Value collaboration.
• Recognize and reward teamwork.
• Inspire others to put service above self.
• Earn respect by respecting others.
• Empower others to be empowered.

employees at full pay for several months after the blaze and then on full benefits after that as the plant was being rebuilt. They could have found jobs with other companies at the time, but they didn't. They stayed available and felt motivated to help him recover from the ashes of catastrophe.

Feuerstein is no saint and no fool, just a good business leader and visionary whose workforce barely doubled from 1982 to 1995 while business more than tripled. To Feuerstein, it was the way he was raised; it was the right thing to do. To savvy managers, it was the quintessential example of enlightened self-interest, a kind of professional selflessness that strengthens relationships and overcomes almost all obstacles. Because Feuerstein cared for his employees, they cared for him.

Unlocking Invention

W. Edwards Deming was a great proponent for driving *fear* out of the workplace. Known for helping reform Japanese management style following World War II, Deming understood how paralyzing fear could be to the creative process within organizations. His concepts of inclusion, continuous process and quality improvement,

The Power of Language

The language that managers use reinforces how employees understand who they are and what they do. At Disney, the department responsible for hiring is known as "central casting" and employees are regarded as "cast members." Visitors to the Disney parks, hotels, and cruise ships are called "guests" and employees treat them accordingly. A manager of a Midwest utility firm is referred to as the "process owner for attracting, developing, and retaining employees." In these examples, language conveys expectations of desired behaviors for organizational members. Such terminology recognizes the special roles individuals play in helping the organization succeed and encourages innovation, play, and personal invention.

and team-based organizational structures led to a renaissance of the Japanese economy and the rise of one of the strongest economic forces in the world during the latter part of the 20th century. His concepts called for less direct supervision, more training, more accountability, and more measurement of desired outcomes.

Deming also believed that merit pay and merit pay plans encouraged short-term performance while annihilating long-term planning. He believed further that merit plans contributed to increased fear in the workplace and nourished politics and rivalry. Certainly, Deming's views are shared by others. And, while most experts agree on the need to recognize performance with appropriate rewards, linking rewards to the performance of a group as a whole and to longer-term productivity goals enhances teamwork.

To unlock innovation, managers must not only treat employees fairly and recognize their contributions, but also pay employees well for their ingenuity and effort. If all the rewards go only to management, employees will soon depart for greener pastures. Beyond the matter of fair and appropriate rewards, smart managers pay careful attention to all aspects of recognizing employees, including how employees are called, what their tasks are termed, and how they refer to the processes and missions for which all are accountable.

Nothing is so rewarding for managers as seeing an environment of aha's, where employees are working together, discovering new ways and new ideas for delivering desired outcomes.

Getting into the "Zone"

Any one who has participated in athletic exercise knows about that "the zone," that point when person and process are one, and the spirit is transported high above the conscious world. Here's how you as a manager can achieve this same state:

• Describe the desirable.
• Create cultures of excellence.
• Embrace employees as "partners."
• Unleash creativity.
• Continuously encourage service.
• Empower others to excel.
• Recognize the right stuff, even right intentions.
• Reward generously.
• Have fun.
• Let aha's happen.

For "Kay Anderson," it was the joy of seeing how employees really took to the concept of self-direction and how differently they went about giving improved levels of care to their clients. For CEO Herb Kelleher, CEO of Southwest Airlines, it has been the "aha" of seeing how a unique culture of fun-loving employees, a thoughtfully integrated system of unique activity sets, and a rigorous process for recognizing and rewarding employees overall has produced one of the top-rated, top-performing airlines in the industry. And for retailer Nordstrom's, it's seeing how customer dedication, employee rewards (typified by a generous commission program), and an empowering culture have produced a reputation for unparalleled customer service and generated strong profits.

Certainly, there are many other organizations where managers have come to realize the hard dollar returns from effective management of the "soft" dollar aspects of their business. Unlocking invention and creativity requires unconventional approaches to conventional problems.

The Efficacy of Values

You are certainly familiar with how organization structures are traditionally depicted using a boxes and lines. But a better means of displaying organizational systems might be a number of concentric circles, with the innermost circle representing the customer. Somewhere between the innermost and outermost circles might be the ring of "administrative support" or the "infrastructure," where managers and systems might logically reside. The outermost circle would clearly have to be reserved for the organization's values or guiding principles or vision. It is this outermost circle that determines how the entire organizational system—represented by all the concentric circles—operates. At Nordstrom's, organizational values represent the Nordstrom way; at Southwest Airlines, the Southwest way; and so on. What values or guiding principles or vision determine how *your* company operates?

Managers make value judgments every day. Usually the principles by which they are guided are personal rather than organizational. But, a more effective way of working is to have a set of clearly articulated values or guiding principles by which everyone can operate.

One way of establishing such criteria is to work with your employees. By crafting a system of values together, everyone gets an opportunity to identify what's important and how decisions will be made in the future. If, on the other hand, a set of organizational values already exists, you can work with your

---

Values Make the Difference

A long-term care facility owned by the Sisters of Charity of Nazareth espouses the following values, which apply to employees and residents alike:

- *Quality.* "We...(serve) with care, compassion, and (concern)."
- *Justice.* "We...respect (people) as they are, protect (their) human rights,...and promote (their) continued development."
- *Collaboration.* "We...work together..."
- *Compassion.* "We commit ourselves (compassionately) to the needs of others."
- *Stewardship.* "We...make the best possible use of our resources in the spirit of our mission."

In an industry marked by unprecedented turnover, these values are key to attracting and retaining employees. Yes, this is an organization run by a religious group, and these principles work everywhere when intelligently applied.

employees to interpret the system and articulate what the values mean for them and how they can be applied as you all work together in the future. Recognizing employees in the values-articulation process is a great way to forge relationships and set future guidance systems that allow each person to be work and interact purposefully and responsibly.

Values permit managers and employees to deal with issues more objectively, rather than subjectively. If there is a debate around how resources will be used in a department or by whom, a principle of "stewardship" allows people to discuss what is the most responsible way to use resources to achieve the greatest good. This approach promotes discussion rather than debate and accords all parties the respect and time to be heard before reaching a final decision.

Establishing the right values is critical. Watching employees work within the boundaries—without management intervention—is highly satisfying. Managing can be very rewarding when you're able to say you're proud of the decisions being made by the people you've nurtured.

Remember: in the convention of concentric circles, it's the outer ring of values and guiding principles that holds the organizational structure together. It's the ring where leadership and direction ultimately reside.

Smart Managing

What Criteria Are Best for Us?

When establishing principles, it's important to select words that convey overarching values that are in the best interest of all parties—employees and customers alike. For example, "mutual respect" conveys the notion that all persons should be treated professionally, with consideration. "Honesty" suggests rigorous truth and probity in all matters, whether large or small. Once the list is complete, do a "test": use a real workplace situation to see how the values influence and guide desired outcomes. If people struggle in discussing the issues, that's good. It means they're substantive. Once you adopt your principles, use them!

As a manager, it isn't possible for you to be everywhere—in every transaction, at every moment, with every employee—nor should you expect that of yourself. A more meaningful use of your time and management talent is in helping to create the outer ring that is ever-present to guide all behavior and decisions. Its existence is a tribute to the way in which you recognize and reward employees by allowing them the opportunity to do the right stuff.

Leading by Example

Your influence as a manager will be felt largely through the example you set. Smart managers know they have to "walk the talk" if they're to have any credibility with employees. If customers are important, then they are important, and everything stops for the customer. If people are valued, then they are valued, and everyone deserves time, attention, and personal respect.

Know that your behavior is constantly being monitored—by your employees and by others. So, don't do anything you wouldn't want to read about in the news. Even when you're behind closed doors, employees have a way of knowing if anything's amiss. Smart managers know that the best course, in the event of problems, is to be open and forthright. It's much less complicated and a lot more authentic.

If People Matter, Then They Matter!

Here are several ways to demonstrate you recognize and value your employees:

- Treat people with respect.
- Be on time.
- Be present in conversations; listen actively.
- Keep employees informed.
- Develop people fully.
- Promote continuous learning.
- Be fair.
- Elicit ideas, suggestions, concerns—and act on them.
- Lavish appreciation.
- Be generous with opportunities—and rewards.
- Affirm the value of others' contributions.
- Be available.
- Respond to employee requests promptly.

Remember: if employees matter, they matter. And it's your job to show it! And this can be one of the most effective forms of recognition.

Adding Value

In the context of strategic initiatives and overall direction, organizational activities are either *primary* or *support* with respect to their alignment with organizational goals and objectives. For example, marketing products and services would be regarded as a primary activity for an organization in the business of selling products and services. The activity of marketing is directly aligned with one of the principal strategies of the organization and, therefore, must be regarded as "adding value." Managing, on the other hand, is not a primary activity for that organization, since the activity of managing is secondary or subordinate to the primary mission of marketing goods and services. Expressed another way, the organization is not in the business of generating income by managing resources internal to the organization. Consequently, although the activity is important, it is nonetheless secondary.

Simply put, if you're a manager, the most important thing you can do for yourself and for your employees is to figure out what it is you do or can do to add value to the organization's reason for being. And, let me suggest, it's not managing other people.

So what is it? Let's say one of the key strategies of the organization is to become an employer of choice. (Wendy's CEO adopted such a strategy in the late 1980s to attract and retain quality people for his restaurants.) Your challenge would then be to determine what you could do to attract and retain quality people. Perhaps you might decide that developing learning experiences for employees not only would make them want to stay with your organization to learn as much as they could, but would also benefit your organization in that employees would become more capable and competent to perform at optimum levels. Or you might decide that implementing team-based organization structures would enable employees to problem solve and serve customers with greater proficiency and speed, resulting in increased sales and improved customer satisfaction. Consequently, organizing and training such employee teams would be a primary or value-adding activity on your part.

> ### Thinking Strategically
> Get a copy of your company's strategic plan. Identify the three, four, or five major strategy action areas. If there isn't a plan, determine what the major strategies might be. Then look at your responsibilities and those of your employees. Determine how you can redesign jobs to add value. Keep the strategies in a prominent location and reference them constantly. Evaluate each action or decision on the basis of whether it adds value to growth of the business, team competence, or the relationship with its customers. Doing this helps you prioritize what's really important.

If you continued with this line of thinking, ultimately you would have to come to the conclusion that, from a strategic perspective, managing is a secondary, non-value-adding function. Yes, it's important, but it does not contribute the kind of return our examples above would provide, i.e., employee retention and increased sales and customer satisfaction.

So, start now to do what other smart managers are doing. Recognize that your employees are the resources your organization is relying upon to make a difference and that it's up to you to determine how best to recognize and reward them for making a significant difference in your business. By doing that, you will be increasing your value as a manager.

Remember: adding value is what it's all about—for you and your employees. If you're not adding value, what are you doing?

Inspiring Excellence

Inspiring excellence calls into play all of the skills and perspectives we've touched upon in this chapter. Michele Hunt, a former Herman Miller executive, writes about "dream makers" who have built businesses and entire communities by choosing a different path from the norm, both for their lives and the people they've inspired.* In almost every instance, the dream makers in her book have a sense about the world beyond their own lives. They take responsibility for that world and have an unwavering belief in being able to overcome any obstacle to making

*Michele Hunt, *Dream Makers: Putting Vision and Values to Work* (Palo Alto, CA: Davies-Black Publishing, 1998).

> **Key Term**
>
> **Excellence** In the world of work, the process of continuous improvement toward some higher standard or state of being. It's different from *perfection*, in that *perfection* represents the highest form of excellence, an ideal state that is unattainable. But the process of adding value continuously is the pursuit of excellence. It is a journey that every manager needs to chart and embark upon with employees of the new workforce.

things better. They share a deep faith in people and revere relationships. They trust the knowledge and judgment of others, as well as their own, and use all information to make decisions that are from their hearts as well as their minds. They build teams, use creativity, learn and grow, and believe deeply they are part of some "invisible wholeness" or "field of energy" that calls them to contribute beyond the limits of their own personal needs and wants.

You might be thinking that you're "just a manager," that you're not the head of an organization, the builder of a community. But why can't you think and act like a dream maker? As the head of your unit or division, which is a small organization and community, you can make a big difference in inspiring excellence.

In a world of indifference, where loyalty and security are *passé*, "free agent" employees need inspiration and a system of beliefs that enables them to excel beyond the boundaries of current assignments and the corporate identities of the moment. Managers of the new workforce understand the value of inspiring excellence. Doing so recognizes the ability each of us has to create something larger than ourselves and focuses on the intrinsic reward of pursuing and providing excellence.

Perhaps there's no better example than that of Mary Kay Cosmetics. Of course, what comes to mind for most people when you mention "Mary Kay" is "pink Cadillacs"—a reward symbol for those salespeople who achieve the highest levels of sales. What most people don't realize is that when Mary Kay Ash founded the organization in 1963, her dream was to offer women "unprecedented opportunities for financial independence, career advancement and personal fulfillment." Her business was not simply cosmetics; it was a vehicle for building the self-esteem of women around the world—employees and customers alike. Most sales representatives earn far less than one might imagine, but they are inspired both personally and professionally by the vision of enhancing self-esteem with the sale of products that are also environmentally friendly.

Helping employees add value, helping them improve their skills, empowering them to take on responsibility and authority for their performance and ability to contribute to the organization, inspiring them to excellence—these are all powerful forms of recognition. They are also the behaviors of leaders who understand that their success is tied to undertaking such actions in a conscious and systematic fashion.

Manager's Checklist for Chapter 4

❏ Power is illusory. Managers who appear "powerful" are so because of how they are respected by others. It's an earned state, brought about by working with and recognizing others as competent, capable, and contributing members of a community.

❏ Leading is inherently rewarding for managers when they begin to see employees succeeding at becoming independent and self-actualized in the pursuit of excellence.

❏ Stewardship is rewarding for employees because they see managers as recognizing and rewarding employees in ways that are far more beneficial and effective than traditional approaches.

❏ Adding value requires total alignment with organizational strategies and direction. By focusing on value-adding opportunities, managers enhance the likelihood of attracting, developing, and retaining the best human resources.

❏ Unlocking creativity and innovation requires driving fear out of the organization. Pay systems, language, management style, organization culture: all contribute to an empowering or a restrictive environment. Savvy managers do everything within their power to create environments that recognize and reward competence.

❑ Managing by values, leading by example, and inspiring excellence are effective ways to influence inspired performance.

organizations, where combative cultures have been a concern. It's not just a good idea to establish and uphold certain principles in your culture; it's a smart policy—and it may even save lives. You don't want to be the manager who makes the headlines for getting shot by some employee who feels devalued, unrecognized, and unrewarded.

If one of the guiding principles you decide to adopt for your culture is, say, "we work as a team" or "we celebrate our unique

Look for the Good in Every Culture

⚠️ **CAUTION!**

Whether merging companies or blending functions, smart managers recognize there's good in every culture—and they praise those aspects that are valuable. Don't make the mistake of believing there's only one right culture or that department A's culture is better than B's. That road leads to "win-lose" destinations, and something of value will be lost—people or ideas, commitment or motivation, something valuable. So look for the good in your culture. Recognize it! Celebrate it! Treasure it! If you appreciate the value of your culture, it will pay off and the others who appreciate that culture will become your partners.

accomplishments," then it must be a living principle in every way. You must look for, recognize, and celebrate every event that epitomizes the cultural elements you want replicated—that's a process of recognition and reward, in and of itself. Also, as a manager of change, you must ferret out the pockets of resistance. Like our CEO in Chapter 3 ("Vision, Mission, Values, and Other Dreams"), if the golden rule is "build self-esteem," be prepared to defend the principle and take tough actions to protect the rights of others.

Companies like UPS and Nordstrom's promote from within—not only to recognize competence and performance but also to perpetuate their cultures. They value traditions, principles, desired ways of working, and other cultural factors that contribute to ongoing success. Smart managers look for the successes in their own organizations that epitomize the kind of culture they desire and extol the virtues and teachings of these successes until they become almost folkloric by their repeated telling. We'll take a closer look at some examples in Chapter 9.

Cultures provide the context for how organizations work. If a culture is encouraging and *constructive*, people will feel less apprehensive about taking prudent risks. They will, instead, strive to achieve increasingly high levels of performance. When managers inspire excellence, as we discussed in Chapter 4, a constructive culture—one that recognizes and rewards—will nurture excellence.

By way of contrast, a *restrictive* culture, one that punishes mistakes or demands compliance, tends to discourage organizational members from taking initiative. Being outstanding can be as dangerous as standing out, and organizational members tend to feel defensive in such cultures and are inclined to act in ways that run counter to the more desirable states of self-actualization and achievement. The point is this: to excel, employees need both constructive cultures and encouraging, humanistic managers.

Constructive cultures are rewarding cultures. Savvy managers understand that the new workplace is one that requires constructive cultures, because such environments recognize not only the work to be done but also the value of people. Such cultures in and of themselves provide "psychic income" for employees. They're energizing, affirming, fun to work in, stimulating, interesting, and challenging.

A culture we might describe as *passive*, on the other hand, tends to focus more on people than results. They generally are non-constructive, i.e., restrictive, because they require compliance and conformity, ironically because they discourage individual initiative by requiring people to be dependent on other people—particularly authority figures.

What we might call *aggressive* cultures are just as restrictive because they value competition and power and are prone to focus on results at the expense of human value. Such cultures differ from high-performance cultures in that aggressive cultures tend to be more task-driven than achievement-oriented. With some entrants to the new workplace described in Chapter 1, aggressive cultures could create time bombs, ready to blow at a moment's notice. Other entrants, particularly free agents, most probably will be averse to joining organizations with such

> **Constructive culture** A culture that encourages risk taking and focuses on performance: managers take actions to reinforce behaviors that lead to high individual, group, and organization performance.
>
> **Passive culture** A culture that focuses on people and individual compliance rather than group or organizational achievement and hopes for the best.
>
> **Aggressive culture** A culture that's focused on individual tasks and internal competition rather than long-term group and organizational performance.
>
> The culture that is most productive and the style that will bring out the best in people is constructive.

cultures because they could imagine themselves being personally and professionally unfulfilled.

Indeed, savvy managers know that to attract and retain the right people, especially in tight labor markets, they have to create constructive cultures. Moreover, constructive cultures produce better results over a longer period of time than restrictive cultures, as we'll discuss below. As a manager, take comfort in knowing that constructive cultures are good for your people, good for your organization, and—purely and simply—good for business.

Outcomes and Results

A useful way to think about cultural differences is in terms of the differences between *outcomes* and *results*. An outcome represents more of a desired state whereas a result represents the completion of a task or achievement of a goal.

Nowhere is this difference more apparent than in the context of an organization's culture. Constructive cultures tend to support outcomes and outcome measurement with an integrated approach that values not only the achievement of desired states but also the people contributing to the process. Results-oriented cultures, on the other hand, tend to promote task completion primarily.

Just as organizations have strategies or strategic areas of emphasis, managers have styles that shape the cultural environment around them. Surveys, including 360° feedback instruments, can be quite effective in determining whether you're

MISTAKE PROOFING

Getting Feedback

There are a number of ways to get feedback about the leadership strategies you're using as a manager and their impact on your employees. Survey processes can be quite effective. You can obtain information and materials from firms specializing in such systems, including *Human Synergistics International* in Plymouth, Michigan (800 622-7584, http://www.humansynergistics.com/) and *Human Factors* in San Rafael, California (888 867-9900). Professionally prepared reports on survey results help pinpoint whether your strategies are working and, if not, what strategies would work better.

influencing employees to produce outcomes or results, making it rewarding for them to work hard, or even using rewards to motivate others in an appropriate way. You may think you know what your impact is on others, but you really don't without some process for collecting *objective* feedback at regular intervals. Such information is vital to determining ultimately the kind of culture you are creating as a manager and whether that culture is conducive to constructive achievement or is inhibiting the creative process.

Collaboration

In the new workplace, models of collaboration will be more prominent than in the past, for several reasons. First, to counter the effects of combative cultural experiences, managers will need new paradigms for minimizing conflict and maximizing cooperative efforts. Second, managers cannot afford the inefficiency of systems that harvest hosts of individual contributors—each in business for herself or himself. Consequently, models of collaboration will ensure more interaction among organizational members. And third, collaborative systems of work facilitate the movement of free agent/employees throughout an organizational system. When people better understand how they're expected to work together, they're more likely to produce desirable outcomes. Inasmuch as free agents will be expected to move around, there will be less inclination to protect "turf," i.e., some arbitrary departmental or functional boundary representing "my department" or "her area." Because collaboration calls into play different skill sets and emotional attributes, people will be more inclined to get right down to work.

Managers of the new workplace understand the value of cultures built on principles of collaboration and teamwork. Such cultures are not only constructive; they are also *self-recognizing*. Organizational members, trained in the skills of teamwork, appreciate, respect, and work with one another, because

> **Collaboration** Cooperation of the highest order. When people cooperate, they generally are working together for a common cause, purpose, or goal. Collaboration incorporates the concept of cooperation, but with the suggestion of cooperation of parties from opposing sides, such as enemies or competitors. Working with enemies certainly requires overcoming extreme differences and, while we hope free agent/employees won't be working with enemies at work, the new workplace will demand cooperation of the highest order.

they know that they must to add value continuously. If they try to go it alone or merely "cooperate" in a group, they will fall short of their full potential. Individual members may compromise their positions or leave something out in the spirit of "getting along." Collaboration, on the other hand, demands that all parties engage fully in the process of delivering what they believe is in their own best interest as well as that of others.

Smart managers understand that some new entrants to the workplace will be skeptical of any sort of organizational packaging that looks like "brainwashing" or "corporate gameplaying."

A Stitch in Time

Commenting on the demise of the textile industry in the United States, an industry executive explained, "The survival of any business depends on collaboration. If, in the course of manufacturing a shirt, a pocket is left off by mistake, by the time someone recognizes the problem down the line and sends it back through the system for correction, the product may have been dyed. So the pocket has to be dyed separately and stitched to the shirt; but then the dyes might not match. In the end our margin of profit will have evaporated, and competition will have produced two or more perfectly good shirts to our one. Without collaboration, we're out of business."

Collaboration Is Not a Luxury!

In the new workplace, smart managers know collaboration is a necessity. Consequently, they:

- Train organizational members in teamwork and problem solving,
- Set compelling goals,
- Communicate extensively with all teams and their members,
- Devise ways to encourage integration and collaboration,
- Recognize teamwork and team contributions,
- Reward collaborative efforts for producing desired outcomes.

Consequently, they are vitally aware of how important it is that strategy, culture, and style be aligned. Equally important will be how organizational members are rewarded. While we've touched upon the problems with reward systems in the past, going forward it will be imperative for reward systems to not only influence the right outcomes but also perpetuate collaborative cultures. The last thing managers want in the new workplace are reward systems that drive internal competition. Today, more than ever before, the survival of any business depends on collaboration.

Job Design

As job classifications continue to be reduced and job responsibilities broadened and made more flexible, the design of employee jobs is becoming increasingly important. Indeed, it is the one area of organizational reengineering where fundamental change is most evident. Gone is the emphasis on progressing up the organizational ladder, as we indicated in Chapter 1. Instead, "career banding" is becoming more the norm, where employees move within the context of a broad array of multi-job or multitasking requirements. Career banding promotes cross-functional problem solving and increased flexibility. In the workplace of the future, employees will be recognized more for the number of skills they exhibit on the job and rewarded for their contributions to the welfare of an organization overall.

How job responsibilities are structured says a lot about the expectations and practices of an organization, including its philosophy with respect to people, its values, its culture, and, ultimately, its reward and recognition systems. Restrictive organizations tend to be very detailed with respect to the minute tasks expected of employees. Everything is spelled out in job descriptions, including the catchall clause stipulating that employees can be asked to

> **Career banding** A system designed to flatten organization structures with respect to job levels, job titles, and employee benefits. The associated compensation system has fewer salary levels and generally wider salary ranges. Each career band is without minimum or maximum salary limits since they are all equal.
>
> *Key Term*

do anything at any time by a supervisor or member of management. By looking at a job description, you can anticipate that recognition will not be abundant and rewards will be limited to direct pay for individual productivity only. Such organizations may believe that it's nice if some "team spirit" pops up every once in a while, but they don't consider it essential to getting the work out.

Compensable factors under career banding can vary according to the key requirements of an organization and the critical skills needed in its workforce. Such factors might include:

- Value-added contributions to the organization
- Measurable outcomes
- Skills developed and used
- Exceptional service
- Problem resolution
- Interpersonal effectiveness
- Flexibility
- Creativity

Smart managers know that configuring job responsibilities properly is critical to helping their employees understand what constitutes success. It also is an effective means for communicating how employees are regarded and how they'll be recognized. An instructional, constructive organization will view employees as an integral part of the business equation and will take every opportunity to recognize its employees. Furthermore, job design in such organizations helps foster an overall awareness that the sum contribution of all employees goes to ensuring the success of the enterprise and that all will share in the credit.

> **Job Design**
>
> Good job design establishes a basis for:
> * Determining key task groups, processes, and outcomes
> * Identifying the critical personal attributes needed to perform successfully
> * Hiring the right people by determining job/person fit
> * Encouraging inclusive behavior—communication, cooperation, collaboration
> * Conveying how employees are regarded by the organization
> * Determining job worth
> * Suggesting how people will be recognized
> * Targeting development opportunities
> * Setting standards and expectations for accepted and exceptional levels of performance
> * Planning, measuring, and rewarding performance
> * Ensuring compliance with legal and quasi-legal requirements, including license and/or worker certification

Smart managers appreciate the value of good job design and the fact that it is the cornerstone for setting expectations, determining job worth, recognizing contributions, and rewarding productive outcomes.

Planning, Performing, and Measuring

As we've indicated, job design is a critical element for determining many factors, including job worth, employee fit, and performance planning and management. And, while work can and should be its own reward, employees need to be adequately and fairly compensated for what they do. Absolutely! Unequivocally!

Performance planning provides the means for determining by what measures people will be compensated and for what outcomes. Psychologically, employees appreciate being able to see a direct link between their work contributions and the pay they receive. Moreover, they expect feedback on their work, their careers, their development needs, and their opportunities. Performance reviews can, if properly carried out, can promote such feedback. Indeed, they provide the basis and ongoing opportunity for constructive communication around work.

In most organizations, performance reviews are conducted within the first 90 days of employment and annually thereafter—though sometimes more frequently. But, all too often, reviews are late, skipped, or completed in a cursory fashion. The message in these instances is "we don't take these seriously."

Smart managers know that's the *wrong* message for employees in the new workplace. They appreciate how important performance reviews can be for supplying feedback to employees and gathering information for how they as managers can help employees perform better. Properly used, the process for planning and reviewing performance can serve as a means for continuous recognition. Managers can recognize their employees by regularly involving them in setting goals at the beginning of each planning cycle and determining where and when performance levels need adjustment along the way. Employees can independently assess their own progress against their goals and get support and recognition from their managers as well. Should the organization use a review system that involves 360° feedback, employees will also get feedback from others, including their peers.

As the workforce continues to become more diversified and employee interests more specialized, managers will need to rely more on performance planning and measurement systems that

---

Performance Reviews: Carrot or Stick?

All too often managers use performance planning and reviews to punish employees for falling short of expectations or for pointing out infrequent slip-ups or errors employees make. All this does is create an adversarial relation between managers and employees. If you're tempted to go down that road, don't! Don't waste your time or your employees'. Feelings of resentment, criticism, and negative energy contribute to performance erosion. Instead, use the process to praise desired performance and recognize jobs well done. Positive reinforcement will do more to influence motivation and stimulate desired outcomes than any other single approach. Be frequent! Be consistent! Be generous! As the old saw goes, "You catch more flies with honey than with vinegar."

are clear, open, legally defensible, and individualized. Performance plans that are based on profiled job responsibilities provide customized planning and performance measurements for employees in the new workplace. Such plans are objective because of the systematic process for determining performance criteria and establishing desired outcomes. Performance plans are valuable tools for ensuring that employees have influence in determining job responsibilities, in setting performance criteria on which rewards are to be based, and ultimately in career decisions and future job assignments. Clearly, they establish the best basis for linking pay to performance, as with pay-for-performance plans.

As you begin to think about recognition and rewards in the new workplace, especially with respect to compensation, understand that employees will need constructive cultures to feel appreciated, recognized, motivated. They will also need to clearly understand what is expected of them and how expectations will relate to their compensation. And, they will need the feedback mechanisms to help them know how they are performing in terms of expectations.

Pay for Performance

Pay-for-performance plans are compensation systems designed to trigger employee motivation to perform by providing incentives for work produced for an organization. Incentive payments can be incorporated into an organization's base pay program—like merit increases—or they can be provided as renewable incentives outside of the base pay program. Usually, more dollars are placed at risk under such programs according to required levels of performance against established goals. Whether "motivating" or not, such plans emphasize the direct correlation between performance and pay.

Traditionally, pay plans—like merit systems—have been managed like entitlement programs, where employees have received annual adjustments to pay, in some cases, just for "showing up and doing their jobs." That will not be the case in "performance" organizations of the future, however, where employees will be held more directly accountable for work outcomes.

In the new workplace, pay will need to be more egalitarian. That doesn't mean everyone gets paid the same amount regardless of work contribution. What that means is people throughout the system have equal opportunity to benefit from the gains overall. No one is having to scramble around looking for the right place for the right money, because everyone is being rewarded fairly. Even today, savvy managers are making pay a non-issue from the outset. They're paying their employees appropriately and competitively from the get-go, so they can stay focused on producing excellent products and services for satisfied customers. The emphasis is on creating the right environment (and that includes fair compensation), and then building from there.

Taking Time

Enlightened managers take time to think about the environment they are creating for employees and how the various elements in that world relate. They take a *systems* approach.

Take pay-for-performance plans, for example. Such plans rarely fail for technical reasons, i.e., because of not having the right measures or the right design; they usually fail because managers lose interest in tracking performance and monitoring the system. They think that, once a reward system is designed, they can forget about it—"We did it, already; now let's move on." But, that's not the case. Such programs must serve as living "systems" with appropriate responses to every stimulus; they must have feedback loops and ongoing adjustment. They require review, communication, planning, and continuous maintenance. And, like any living system, without proper care and attention, such programs wither and eventually die from neglect.

Alternatively, such systems fail if managers do not buy into them and then circumvent the program by paying everyone equally or providing "overrides" to the system to reward special-interest employees or punishing others. Or they fail if the programs are exclusively "manager owned and operated." In other words, if managers don't trust employees to be intelligent enough and able to help maintain the programs, then the programs will falter because they're unable or slow to adapt to ever-changing conditions and external challenges. In any event, whether such

Learn and Grow

TRICKS OF THE TRADE

Smart managers know there's no cutting corners when it comes to promoting performance. To ensure everyone is "on board" and aware of what's expected, they:

- Learn, along with their employees, how to set realistic and measurable goals;
- Collaborate in the design and planning of needed performance systems;
- Ensure they know how the various plans work;
- Teach their employees how to excel and use such tools successfully;
- Preserve the integrity of their plans and programs by complying with their intended purpose;
- Encourage peak performance and maximum reward.

programs fail through neglect, abuse, or lack of employee input, the fact remains that the culture of the organization, its values system, and time commitment determine their fate.

In the new workplace, employee involvement is a must, whether it's in planning and measuring individual and group performance or in monitoring a pay-for-performance program. To operate successfully, any system requires all of its resources to be engaged—at one time or another—and that takes time.

For a variety of reasons, as we'll discuss in the following section, few organizations have been willing to move to open-book management programs, in which employees are educated in the financial and operational dimensions of their organization. Probably the two most significant reasons are that it requires a culture of trust and it takes time—time to teach, time to train, time to communicate, and time to see the results. But the payback for organizations that have adopted open-book management as a philosophy and way of doing business has been significant. Managers in such organizations recognize the competence of their people by treating them like responsible adults with a stake in the success of their organizations.

Limits, Structure, and Other Symbols of Caring

Our CEO in Chapter 3 whose organization values "self-esteem" acknowledges the difficulty of communicating in a team-based environment, particularly where people feel empowered to work

at making a difference. "When you've got all that energy flow-
ing, it's a challenge for any manager to stay close to what the
teams are doing and to be available, as a professional resource,
to their needs," he asserts. "At the same time, you've got to set
the direction to ensure everyone is aligned with where the
organization is headed in order to remain competitive in the
marketplace." Indeed, setting direction creates structure and
boundaries within which organizational members can operate.

Structure in today's workplace tends to look like this:

- Well-defined processes, rather than boxes and lines,
  functions, or departments
- Increased accountability and responsibility at a team
  level
- Disciplined routines for conveying information, learning,
  and teaching
- Open systems that include feedback and adjustment to
  customer needs
- Performance standards, planning, and measurement
- Continuous communication and honesty
- Genuine caring and concern—for products, processes,
  and people
- Values and principles by which everyone can work
  together

As organizations continue to flatten their structures and
empower teams, smart managers are recognizing the need for a
disciplined approach to leading and supporting their people.
Traditionally, managers have "cared for" their employees. Not
too long ago, for example, benefits programs were designed
with only a limited number of employee options. Generally,
what applied to one employee applied to all. After all, management knew what was good for employees. They weren't consid-
ered sophisticated enough to appreciate the risk associated with
the stock market, so management made investment decisions
with respect to savings plans. And, of course, some employees
might not understand the importance of life insurance, so
everyone had to have some amount—there was no opting out.

What Constitutes Caring?

Ever wonder what constitutes "caring"? Consider the "good old days" when the doctor withheld vital information from the patient—like "you're going to die." Usually, with family support, the patient might be sheltered from the harsh reality. Today, all that's changed. Patients want the information—even if it's bad news—so they can decide what to do next. If you're tempted to question as a manager how best to "care" for your employees, choose "responsible caring" by giving them information they need as well as a clear review of how the organization is doing and not limiting what they know, working under the false assumption that holding on to information is a way to preserve your power and responsibility.

Employees were lulled into accepting that managers would do the "heavy lifting," make all the tough decisions, and simply tell them what they wanted the employees to do. To perpetuate this approach, long-term employees were given service pins, retirees were rewarded with gold watches, providers of outstanding customer received plaques, etc. Not to say that such symbols weren't appropriate, but rather that they weren't enough. There was little call for employees to take initiative or get involved in the inner workings of the organization.

Most significantly, employees were "protected" from *information*. And so, when hard times hit, employees were surprised by layoffs, loss of benefits, and other takeaways, because they had no idea that conditions were so grave.

One of the most meaningful symbols of responsible caring in the new workplace is an "open book." In reality it's a concept of information sharing that has become a revolutionary shot in the arm for many organizations. One of the most dramatic cases involves Springfield Remanufacturing Corporation, an engine remanufacturer that over a nine-year period from 1983 to 1992 saw sales increase more than fivefold—from $13 million to $70 million—and an initial equity investment of $100,000 grow to more than $23 million in value. The company was created when the plant was purchased from International Harvester by plant management and its employees.

Open-book manage-
ment has been successfully
used by other companies,
including Physician Sales
and Service, Allstate
Insurance, and Pace
Industries. But many com-
panies and their managers
are reluctant to move in this
direction, because "the
information is confidential"
or "it may get out to the
competition" or "employees
don't need to know every-
thing." And, even though
information is the lifeblood

> **Open-book management**   *Key Term*
> The concept of opening the
> financial books to employees and
> sharing operational information.
> Employees are then trained to under-
> stand the significance of the information,
> how to interpret it, and how to measure
> the financial value of their work to orga-
> nizational performance. Trust is at the
> core of open-book management. The
> concept was introduced by Jack Stack of
> Springfield Remanufacturing Corpora-
> tion, who concluded the only way the
> company could be successful was with
> the collective intelligence and commit-
> ment of its employees.

of every organizational system, not everyone believes in open-
book management or full disclosure. Usually, managers are
inclined to "share" information only if it's good, but even in that
instance, the picture they give is not always complete.

Savvy managers understand that trust is a prerequisite to
teamwork and that in the new workplace the way in which information is handled will be highly symbolic of how managers view
employees and highly indicative of future success. If information
sharing is expansive, employees will feel more inclined to stretch
and grow. If, on the other hand, information is restricted, there
will be less of an inclination to feel fully committed.

Time to Kill Time   *Tricks of the Trade*

The new plant manager decided to tap into employee issues to
determine how best he could raise morale. Along the way he
learned that office employees were extremely unhappy with having to
punch in on the new time clock that had been installed just prior to his
arrival. "It's insulting," one employee said. Not long after that, employees
arrived at work to find the clock gone; in its place were time sheets.
Returning to his office that afternoon, he found a big note of thanks from
his employees for trusting them enough to "kill" the time clock.

Certainly, pink Cadillacs, service pins, letters of commendation, and wall plaques are symbols of recognition and appreciation, but they fall far short of true caring. Let's face it: if your boss withheld information from you that could potentially impact your job, what would that say about how he or she recognizes, trusts, and respects you?

Recognizing and rewarding employees in the new workplace requires caring, open communication, discipline, and structure. For an organization to produce desired outcomes, smart managers know that culture, strategy, structure, style, and symbols have to fit together seamlessly. They have to be fully aligned and completely congruent to spark the flames of enthusiasm and motivation.

Manager's Checklist for Chapter 5

❑ Culture is the organizational environment and influences whether employees feel unleashed or restricted with respect to personal performance. Constructive cultures are the most desirable for providing optimum recognition and reward.

❑ Styles of management influence employee motivation. Instructional styles tend to be more empowering than restrictive styles.

❑ Inclusive approaches to setting performance standards and planning outcomes are the best. Plans that are well thought out provide objective measures by which employees can assess their own performance.

❑ Performance plans are excellent vehicles for ongoing communication around performance and performance improvement, all of which takes time. Used properly, they are constructive, empowering, and highly effective in promoting performance.

❑ Collaboration and information sharing in the new workplace are central to the success of every employee.

Recognition as a "Whole Person" Experience

Recognition is a "whole person" experience, not only for the employee but for the manager as well. In Chapter 4, we talked about leadership, stewardship, and various ways caring managers inspire excellence. In Chapter 5, we discussed the importance of building the right environment and culture. Now, we will go deeper into the subject of YOU—the manager: your needs, your wants, and your motives.

"Odd," you might say, given that this is a book about recognizing and rewarding *others*. But not so odd when you consider that *leaders who inspire others lead from the inside out.*

"Know thyself," the admonishment of the Greek oracle inscribed at Delphi, was intended to challenge pilgrims to the ancient site seeking advice. And for centuries the maxim has been reiterated by others and adapted in myriad ways. In *Hamlet* William Shakespeare expressed it as follows: "This above all else: To thine own self be true, and it will follow, as the night the day, thou canst not then be false to any man." A few decades later, Philip Massinger wrote in *The Bondman*, "He that would govern others first should be the master of himself." And Richard

Wright in *Native Son* wrote, "Men can starve from a lack of self-realization as much as they can from a lack of bread."

Enlightened managers lead from the heart as well as the head. Some rely on intuition and enthusiasm to show their caring and concern for people, while others arrive at the heart through personal vulnerability and experiences that enable them to show authenticity and passion. Either way, managers "in the know" about themselves have a strong sense of self and a healthy ability to accept who they are unconditionally. In turn, they're able to see into the hearts of others and touch them "where they live."

If you have any doubt, recall the most accepting, encouraging, affirming person in your formative years—perhaps a grandparent or older friend—and reflect upon the characteristics of that person. Ultimately, you'll come to the one quality that underlies every other constructive attribute, *unconditional love.*

Trite as it may sound, the best managers *love* people. And they find joy in connecting and influencing others to act out of a sense of enlightened self-interest for themselves as well as for others.

Most managers, if asked whether they need recognition to do their jobs, would probably answer, "No." Practically all regard themselves as rugged individualists. After all, in the United States, it's part of our cultural heritage. On the other hand, if asked whether they like recognition, the answer is usually a resounding "Yes!" But, according to a Kepner-Tregoe study, only about 40% of North American workers said they receive any recognition for doing a good job, while the same percentage indicated they receive no recognition at all. In the same study, only 50% of managers said they give recognition for exceptional performance. Apparently, all other performance goes unrecognized as though it were expected and, therefore, unremarkable.

Be rigorously honest with yourself in asking if and how you recognize others. James M. Kouzes and Barry Z. Posner, authors of *Encouraging the Heart: A Leader's Guide to Rewarding and Recognizing Others* (San Francisco: Jossey-Bass Publishers, 1999), developed the "Encouragement Index," a self-assessment

Rooted in Insight

Smart
Managing   Encouraging managers understand the importance of know-
ing who they are, what they stand for, what values are cen-
tral to their lives, and what motivates them to achieve. To be effective
and influential in moving others to action, it's imperative to know what
motivates you personally as a manager. For example, do you like it
when others:
• Respect your abilities?
• Value your opinion?
• Include you in what's happening?
• Show trust in you as a person?
• Appear motivated by your values?
• Tell others about their "great manager"?
   If any of these things matter to you, then you appreciate recognition.

instrument for managers to determine how effective they are in
the motivational aspects of their leadership. The index was born
out of their belief that managers need to "lead from the heart" by
exhibiting behaviors that encourage others. And they're quick to
point out the root meaning of "encouragement" comes from the
Latin word for "heart." Sample challenges from their extensive
index include (pp. 36-37):

  • Expressing high expectations about what people are
    capable of accomplishing.
  • Communicating clearly personal values and professional
    standards to everyone on the team.
  • Finding opportunities to let people know the *why* behind
    whatever they are doing.
  • Personally congratulating people for a job well done.

   Smart managers know the value of these behaviors—for
themselves and for the people they are entrusted to lead.

Honoring the Person Within Others

America's workplace is changing—a truism no one can deny.
Many of the ways in which it is changing have been highlighted in
Chapter 1. And, while much of management's time has focused
on attracting and retaining younger workers, the phenomenon of

an aging population, in particular, is being ignored. As noted in Chapter 1, the aging of the U.S. population presents serious challenges to discerning managers.

Moreover, with emphasis in the 1980s and 1990s having been on downsizing, outsourcing, and expense reduction, disillusioned employees are looking for ways to escape the uncertainty and anxiety of corporate life today. Beverly Goldberg, vice president of The Century Foundation, coauthor of *Corporation on a Tightrope* (New York: Oxford University Press, 1996), and author of *Dynamic Planning: The Art of Managing Beyond Tomorrow* (New York: Oxford University Press, 1994), asserts, "Corporate America will have to reinvent itself to make the workplace a better fit with the needs of all employees, especially older workers, if it expects to survive the graying of America."

At the same time, Generation X workers, those in their mid-20s and 30s, are searching for a deeper meaning to life—something beyond the accretion of wealth and "work for work's sake." Values, principles, even *spirituality* hold greater sway in their lives than mere material accumulation. And Generation Y workers, as we referenced in Chapter 1, are largely focused on their own agenda of self-gratification.

With all of these changes in worker attitudes and the current and future migration of workers from the workplace, it's logical to ask, "Where will needed workers come from?" and "Whose responsibility is it to worry about getting and keeping workers?" Well, the answer to the latter question is *you*, the manager. It's no wonder being a manager in today's workplace can be so stressful—and so isolating. And the answer to the first question is, of course, "It's *your* responsibility to figure that out."

Enlightened managers understand they have to help individuals seeking a balance between a personal and sometimes spiritual path and the realities of the job. And they must address the feelings of alienation and uncertainty that exist in all of us. Doing that is difficult, especially where those in corporate leadership roles may not have awakened to the problems of disparate employee attitudes and values or the importance of feelings. But there are specific things you can do as a manager to

> **⚠ CAUTION! ⚠**
>
> ### There's No Magic Elixir
>
> If you think there's one easy formula or a single approach to recognizing employees, think again. Each worker comes to the workplace with different expectations, wants, and personal values. Experience in the workplace further shapes what each has brought to the table. Smart managers know they must come to understand these differences and address each person according to his or her unique perspectives. The only constant on which you can rely as a manager is your ability to be open, encouraging, and creative in supporting and influencing others in the new workplace.

develop the right kind of perspective for recognizing and rewarding your employees. The key lies in respecting each person based on his or her unique differences.

Look for ways to honor and nurture the whole person. As Alan Briskin writes in *The Stirring of Soul in the Workplace* (San Francisco: Berrett-Koehler Publishers, 1998), p. 67:

> There is no greater challenge to the soul than the forces of authority and (those who) seek its surrender. (Their) immense power ... to demand conformity and inhibit access to (one's) own experience is rooted in the power of ideas and the organizational structure that shapes and organizes these ideas.

In other words, when powerful managers overwhelm others and deny them their claim to cherished traditions, family heritage, and personal experiences, the "overwhelmed" cease to give of themselves. They refrain from revealing who they are and who they can be. They lose their "voice," their essence, their soul—they don't feel in any way recognized—and in the process everyone loses, including managers. They withhold their ideas and their unique contributions and adapt to the will of those who appear more powerful—all in the name of survival. Encouraging the heart requires that you as a manager "honor" the whole person, not just the mechanical know-how of the individual.

Inspirational managers understand the frailty of the human soul and feel the honor of being a steward to their employees.

Like soldiers who follow their leader through enemy territory, employees respond best to the voice of a manager who has

> ### Respecting and Valuing Others
> Honoring the whole person requires insight and learning
> through experience. Smart managers, leading in a complex and
> changing workplace:
> • Respect the service of those who have toiled long in the trenches.
> • Value the spirituality of those who thirst for life's meaning.
> • Recognize the pursuit of happiness by those who seek gratification.
> • Understand the hunger of those striving to make ends meet.
> • Divine innovative ways to reveal joy and fulfillment in the shared
>   experience of "creating."
> • Celebrate the gifts and "voices" of all who labor.
>   Anthony Robbins, author, consultant, and seminar leader, begins
> every formal engagement by saying, "It's an honor to be with you."
> Even though others pay for his expertise or pay to hear him speak, *he*
> is the one who expresses *honor* at being called. He seems to under-
> stand helping others gives meaning to his life.

their survival and their well-being at heart. Smart managers
know instinctively that they cannot even contemplate any
undertaking, any "battle," any "enemy engagement" without the
support of their people. Moreover, the spirit, heart, and soul of
the followers must be intact, if they are to rise to the challenge.

Rites of Recognition

Few examples of rituals of initiation exist in our American society,
and yet such rites are extremely important. They mark passages
from the stage of the uninitiated and untested to that of the initiated and proficient. They signal readiness for more advanced experiences and symbolize acceptance into a larger community. Rites
of initiation are primal forms of recognition of achievement,
acceptance, actualization, celebration. Such processes convey a
certain set of standards that members must meet before advancing to the next level. They also convey respect for those who
have been initiated in the past, and they help to establish continuity and a certain connection between generations. Indeed, the
process of ritualistic initiation enhances individual and group self-
esteem by recognizing organizational traditions and the unique
qualities and developmental stages of the initiates.

In an organizational context, rudimentary rites exist in various forms. For example, when new employees complete an orientation program and are assigned to their work post, a type of passage has occurred; but for the most part, there's little or no celebration and scant recognition. Candidly, the way an organization orients new hires says a lot about what it does and does not value in the organizational community and in its people.

Other examples of initiation include:

- Mastering desired skills for which compensation levels have been set, i.e., as with skill-based pay programs
- Achieving certification, e.g., CPA, LCSW, etc.
- Promoting to positions of greater responsibility
- Attaining certain milestone years of service
- Retiring

Yet, even in these examples, there is little or no ritualistic recognition, celebration, acclamation. Indeed, these are missed opportunities in any number of organizations. Not so with organizations like Disney, Mary Kay Cosmetics, or Rohm & Haas of Kentucky. Quite the opposite, as we'll discuss below. Of course, not all rites of initiation are of a positive nature; some can come as trials by fire, but they're still worthy of recognition.

Smart managers understand the importance of rituals. Rather than considering them to be frivolous activities or a waste of time, they view such ceremonial celebrations as a means for conveying what is important about their area of responsibility, their organization, their team. Such occasions also provide powerful opportunities to recognize and formally welcome individuals into a new community, department, team, or organization. One of the most obvious occasions for ritualistic celebration is upon the completion of any formal orientation process for employees who are new to an organization, as we'll discuss below.

There's been lot of ground shifting in the American workplace over the last few years, as many Americans have been uprooted from the jobs. In the new workplace, you will be challenged as a manager to make fertile the ground on which you

Know Your Rites

Consider every opportunity that can be reframed into a rite of initiation. Identify the values associated with passing from uninitiated to initiated states. Pick symbols and ceremonial practices to mark the event in everyone's mind and connect the newly initiated in some way with those who have gone before them. Such opportunities could include:

• Completing an orientation process
• Landing a new account
• Achieving designated levels of performance
• Moving into a new area of business
• Completing certification requirements
• Discovering a new process or product improvement
• Satisfying a valued customer

are building the future. One of the most effective ways in which to do that is by symbolizing, ritualizing, and recognizing excellent work, exemplary behavior, and enterprising employees. Savvy managers look for opportunities to create new "roots" every day, and ritual is one of the most effective tools for initiating, recognizing, and assimilating people into the traditions of the initiated.

Preparing for "Them"

Have you ever noticed what expectant parents do to prepare for the arrival of a newborn? They identify and decorate a bedroom. They buy "stuff"—children's furniture, toys, clothes, car seats, dishes, diapers, anything and everything you can imagine for the little person. And, if there are other children in the family, the parents instruct them as to what they'll need to do or how they can help mommy or daddy with the new arrival. All those preparations show that there's something special about a new arrival. Now contrast that picture with how many organizations prepare for new employees.

Most employee turnover comes within the first year of employment, and some of the highest is often within the first few months. Few organizations prepare for new hires as if they were preparing to take on a new baby—and yet they should. It's not the same of course, but there are some common principles at work. Oftentimes, new employees are rushed through the process of "enrollment" for payroll and benefits purposes (euphemistically called "orientation") and then they're thrust into the pool of "sink or swim." There, incumbents—usually stressed by work demands and a lack of resources—view the new arrivals as inconveniences who are going to interfere with their routines, often making them feel at least uncomfortable and sometimes downright unwelcome. Within a short time, the new hire is forced to leave or "get with the program." No mentoring, no company history, no ritual, no celebration: just "hit it"!

In the new workplace, where free agent/employees feel disaffected, where turnover rates are high, and where new social contracts are being forged, nothing could be more important than the process by which employees are assimilated into their organizations. Values-driven managers understand the significance of the orientation process and celebrate its completion by new entrants with great displays of public acceptance and welcome. It is one of the first rites of passage: it permits recognition of employees early on in their employment relationship and it sets the tone for others to follow.

Savvy managers understand that tomorrow's workforce is coming from educational institutions where violence and the threat of harm may loom large. With many new employees feeling apprehensive about working in organizations and about personal safety, it is incumbent upon managers to recognize these concerns and make sure the workplace is safe. Your

> **Peer Ownership**
> At Rohm & Haas of Kentucky, an industrial chemical plant owned by a global giant headquartered in Philadelphia, team members are trained in interviewing job candidates. Recognizing the right skills and abilities is important to the team and plant safety. Once a successful candidate is hired, co-employees have a vested interest in her or his success. The new hire comes to the organization fully recognized and valued at the outset. Orientation is a step-by-step training experience that extends for more than a year. Want to minimize mistakes and maximize recognition? Try peer interviewing.

job in this regard will be difficult, because employees may have encountered other organizations where safety and personal growth were given lip service but not much else. However, if you enlist the help and understanding of co-employees and team members, then everyone will appreciate the significance of these new people and be appropriately prepared for their arrival. (Of course, this advice is appropriate for preparing for new hires who are not coming straight from educational institutions, as well.)

Recognition for employees should begin even before the new hires cross the threshold. But, with every passage from uninitiated to initiated, remember to celebrate, commemorate, ritualize, and recognize the special resources you have to manage—"people."

Celebrating Life

Like the Fiddler on the Roof, recognizing employees should be like celebrating life. James Kouzes and Barry Posner give a wonderful example of how best to recognize employees in *Encouraging the Heart* (p. 16). The story comes from *In Search of Excellence: The Video*, and it tells how Tom Melohn of North American Tool and Die presents—with great showmanship—a Super Person award, dubbed the "Freezer" award, for employee Kelly, who contrived an ingenious way to fit a metal rod into a cylinder by freezing the rod to shrink it. The result was avoiding having to reject the part in the context of a "no reject" environment. Melohn has Kelly retrieve the award from a freezer in front of his peers and takes the opportunity to recognize and reward Kelly while reminding onlookers of the standard of no rejects. The whole scene is done in good fun and personal friendship, as Melohn puts his arm around Kelly to express his appreciation.

Savvy managers have a flair for recognizing others! They also understand that more creativity and energy are exhibited in environments that are fun. They view fun as not only healthy, but also profitable. Discovery is viewed as a journey; mistakes, a means to learning; and learning, a means to growth.

Imagine what would have happened to Ivory soap if some over-controlling manager had rejected the product because it had too much air in it. It wasn't supposed to float! It took a creative marketing department to craft the right "spin" and, lo and behold! floating was transformed into an attribute of purity. The "wrong" glue at 3M made Post-it® Notes one of the company's most notable successes. Vodka was popularized in the U.S. by its promoters, who claimed it would "leave you breathless" and "take your breath away" because it left no odor on your breath. All are excellent examples of outcomes that originated from innovation and having fun.

Creative, fun-loving managers recognize employees in unique ways, like Melohn of North American Tool and Die. Here are some of the ways you might think about for recognizing employees with fun and fanfare:

- Celebrate the achievement of team goals with co-employees and management.
- Communicate individual and group accomplishments.
- Tell others; tell customers; tell the world. It's good business, and people love the recognition.
- Celebrate certain lengths of service, e.g., 5, 10, 15, and more years. But don't do it with standard dinners and routine presentations. Really tell what employees have contributed and why you value them. It serves a dual purpose—for the employees being recognized and those aspiring to gain recognition.
- Celebrate success of every kind—and even constructive failures. Have fun!
- Rejoice over personal events, e.g., birthdays, marriages, births—you know, life!
- Enjoy the company of your employees by walking around, watching for the "wins," and taking pleasure in others having fun.

Celebrations are occasions for recognition and commemoration. They require public expression: assemblies, notices, festivities—anything you can think of to acknowledge with ritual and ceremony. Such events serve to communicate a standard as well as to recognize people who achieve and exceed expectations. In today's environment of doing more with less and stress, stress, stress, celebration of life goes a long way to helping people lighten up. So, have a ball!

The Whole Person

Christopher Reeve, alias Superman, actor, activist, and vice chairman of the National Organization on Disability, commented recently on how people often stand alongside him at his shoulder to talk to him. Because he uses a wheelchair and is a quadriplegic, he is unable to turn his head to see them, so he has to ask them to walk around to the front of the chair where he can see them. "It's as if they are uncomfortable being with someone who is disabled. They're afraid to look at the person," according to Reeve.

This is a phenomenon shared by 53 million disabled Americans. But, how many others who are not disabled share the same experience, when others fail to look at them and see them as a whole person? Bree Walker, a news anchor for KNSD TV in San Diego, has hands without digits. Still her presence is commanding and her mind is powerful. She comments, "30% of Americans in the workplace fail to socialize with, that is, talk to or even acknowledge someone who is disabled." Similarly, non-disabled workers have experienced the same behavior—perhaps even from some manager. Caring managers are not afraid to go

---

⚠ CAUTION!

Check the Intent

Here's a list of caveats to ensure your celebrations are constructive:

- Don't use humor to communicate veiled threats or to mask anger.
- Don't crack jokes at others' expense.
- If you have to tell jokes about anyone, make sure you're the subject of the jest. It will make you appear more authentic and you won't risk hurting someone's feelings.
- Don't make others uncomfortable. Celebrate in good taste.
- Don't roast. Build self-esteem.

If in doubt, check your intent. If it's not linked to building pride and improving performance, don't do it.

What Price Acceptance?   ⚠ CAUTION! ⚠

Resourceful managers ensure that individual identities are not being repressed and that the individual and collective genius of all are recognized and rewarded. For example, Betty Bayé, writer for *The Louisville Courier-Journal*, says, "You'd be amazed at what Black people give up to fit in at work. They can't talk about their weekends, what music they listen to, or even what they like to eat. They have to deny a part of who they are to be accepted." As an African-American female, Bayé understands what energies, ideas, and enthusiasm are being lost to the American workplace.

---

looking for the talents and abilities that lie within every human being. Indeed, they strive to see the whole person and not just some aspect that is only a part of the whole.

Visionary managers revere relationships and are fearless about looking into the eyes of others to see the whole person— even if some of the parts are flawed or the whole is less than perfect—and are equally fearless about being open with others, about being a whole person, however flawed and imperfect.

Empowerment

Dona Airey, a licensed clinical social worker, and her colleague, Patricia Keown, were demonstrating the power of visual imaging at a workshop entitled "Giving Voice to Your Self." They asked participants to pair off, facing one another. One member from each pair extended his hand straight out in front of his body, palm down, while the person opposite extended his hand, placing his palm directly on the back of his partner's hand. The first member was then asked to envision an extremely positive moment in his life—some happy occasion on which he'd felt particularly joyful.

On cue, the first member lifted his hand steadily and firmly, while his partner pushed down hard upon the outstretched hand. Within about 20 seconds, Dona called time. Most hands remained extended straight out; in fact, some had pushed upward enough to break the press. After a brief rest, the pairs faced off again. This time the first member was asked to envision a very sad occasion in his life. On cue, the first member pressed his hand upward while his partner exerted downward pressure. In less than 20 seconds, almost all hands were deflected downward. During the debriefing, the second member of each pair reported feeling more energy and strength from his or her partner while the partner was envisioning positive images and less when envisioning negative ones.

Later in the workshop, Dona and her colleague asked participants to reflect and journal about a time in their lives when they might have "lost their voice." For some it was during a marriage to a partner who subordinated the will of his or her mate. For others it was an employment situation, e.g., working for a boss with a repressive management style or losing a job. Almost everyone in the workshop could recall a situation in which he or she felt powerless. Participants were then asked to reconstruct the situation mentally and envision constructive ways in which they could have retained or recovered their voice. Envisioning a desired outcome and being encouraged to implement their plans, participants were generally motivated to move toward implementing positive change in their lives and avoid losing power in such situations in the future.

> **Key Term**
>
> **Empowerment** Giving authority or control to another. Restrictive managers often resist the concept of empowering employees because they labor under the illusion of having more control than they actually do. Enlightened managers understand that empowering works in at least two ways: it can provide responsibility and accountability for something and it encourages others to feel powerfully enabled to achieve challenging objectives.

Managing in the new workplace demands empowerment, not only because new entrants are resistant to autocratic styles of control, but also because empowerment works—and the results are eminently more beneficial. Envisioning desired outcomes in today's workplace is akin to setting high standards and having a manager who expresses confidence in the ability of employees by saying, "I know you can do it." But each employee needs to find his or her own voice, if it has been suppressed. Organizations cannot afford to have employees contributing less than they are able or desire to. Therefore, it benefits everyone to think constructively and for managers to encourage employees and empower them with challenging goals, full accountablity, and continuous recognition if you want to get the most from everyone.

Choosing Collaboration

In Chapter 5 we discussed the necessity for collaboration and teamwork in the new workplace. Strategy, structure, culture, and style must be aligned to foster collaboration. But, *structure follows strategy*. By that we mean that organizational structure must align with the stated strategies of the organization. If teamwork and synergy are desired states, then all structure must be consistent with that strategy.

Collaboration also recognizes the value of people and the individual differences and talents they bring to the table. Collaborative systems represent the highest form of structural recognition, above traditional command-and-control structures with "one employee/one boss" reporting relationships. In the new workplace, relationships are more networked—both structurally and electronically.

Without structures to serve as connections, no employee or group of employees can be totally effective. As we've noted, structures must serve the needs of people and not the other way around. With the right structures, employees can "choose" to collaborate more readily, because systems and processes

Structure Architecture in its broadest sense—the configuration of working and reporting relationships, work processes, policies and procedures, orientation programs, work standards, information architecture, communications protocols, project designs, work assignments, position profiles, job design, compensation schemes, recognition systems, processes for decision making and problem solving, organizational values, training and development programs, work processes, performance plans, and personal goals. In other words, everything that serves to connect people and resources and coordinate how work gets done in an organization.

are designed to encourage it. And it's in the choosing that people feel motivated, empowered, and recognized. Their thoughts and ideas are recognized by others and they, in turn, recognize others' thoughts and ideas.

Collaboration must be structured to ensure optimum working relationships and maximum effectiveness. Smart managers know that collaborative structural designs allow employees to gain the greatest advantages from their diversity and promote win-win solutions. They minimize conflict, as noted in Chapter 5, and recognize the whole person.

Moreover, reward systems, in and of themselves, must support collaborative working relationships. They must be structured to facilitate teamwork and minimize internal competition among co-employees. In the new workplace, reward systems must encourage synergy, collaboration, and creative problem solving. Compensation practices and performance appraisal systems must be fair and equitable, and they must recognize and engage the whole person.

For new entrants into the workplace, collaboration offers a viable approach to conflict resolution. For those seeking spirituality in their lives, collaboration provides a model of peacemaking. For those seeking personal gratification, collaboration offers a more pleasurable way of working. For employees and managers alike, collaboration is the most effective model for engaging the whole person.

Discovery Is a Continuous Journey

Savvy managers understand full well that organizational systems, compensation programs, and pay philosophies are continuing to evolve. Any number of "experiments" are under way in the American workplace, such as with skill-based pay or pay for knowledge programs, gainsharing plans, and pay-for-performance programs. We'll discuss these in more detail in Chapters 9 and 10.

Such systems are not static. They can ill afford to be. They continue to change and evolve as conditions change. But, in the context of the new workplace, one thing is very apparent to dis-

---

Choosing to Collaborate

Employees choose to collaborate when:
• The philosophy around interpersonal relations is "win-win."
• Managers structure time for purposeful communication and the mutual sharing of concerns, issues, and ideas.
• Organizational structures facilitate working together.
• Trust and respect are valued principles.
• Processes are available for mediation of personal differences.
• Managers recognize both the individuals and the collaborative means they use to achieve results.
• All participants share proportionately in the rewards.
• The focus of attention is on employees rather than management.
• Managers personally exhibit collaborative behavioral and thinking styles.

---

cerning managers: organizational structures, recognition systems, and reward programs must meet the needs of the whole person. If the intent behind plan designs is merely to find new and better ways to extract human, intellectual, and emotional intelligence at the expense of the whole person, no one wins!

While newer concepts in compensation, such as skill-based pay, appear more aligned with personal needs, these systems are not standalone. Other pay programs must be implemented to link pay with performance. Unlike traditional compensations systems that value technical ladders and maturity curves, as in legal and educational professions, skill-based pay systems encourage employees to acquire a broad range of knowledge and ability. One thing is for certain: discovery is a continuous journey. No one person or manager, no one expert or organization has all the answers. Designing effective reward and recognition systems requires that managers:

• Involve the "customers," namely, the employees who are recipients and "consumers" of the systems.
• Monitor employee satisfaction and performance effectiveness on an ongoing basis.
• Willingly change and adopt systems to be more responsive to the needs of employees.

Skill-Based Pay

An experiment in skill-based pay has been in progress at General Mills in its Squeezit business since the late 1980s. To minimize risks associated with entering a new business, the company engaged in an experiment involving a participative approach to managing the business, an ongoing organization design process, and a pay-for-skills concept that was open to modification as needed. Compensation was intended to encourage employees to develop skills required for successful performance, although pay was not directly linked to performance. Compensation levels and satisfaction ratings over time were reportedly higher than with traditional programs.

- Strive to recognize, reward, and encourage development of the whole person.
- Provide sound bases that are in the best interests of both their employees and the organizations for which they work.

In a workplace that can be potentially dispirited by the events of the day as well as the past and challenged by the diversity of interests, values, and abilities of its people today and in the future, recognition must be a whole-person experience. Savvy managers understand that "control" is spiritually deadening. They recognize the need to encourage and develop employees and, to some extent, assist with healing of the vulnerabilities in our midst. If you are committed to search, if you are willing to innovate, if you are open to discovery, your journey will be fruitful and exciting. You will find myriad ways to speak to the heart of your people every day—and *you* will be encouraged in the process!

Manager's Checklist for Chapter 6

❑ Know yourself. Be certain you know how you relate to your employees and the various ways in which you can and should recognize them and their endeavors.

❑ Recognition is a "whole person" process. Engage the head, heart, hands, and spirit of your employees by relating and responding to their interests and needs.

❏ Celebrate accomplishments and the process of "initiation" by ritualizing achievements. Tying ceremony to standards provides recognition to honorees and benchmarks for others.

❏ Empowerment is the highest form of recognition in the workplace. Provide opportunities for employees to shine.

❏ Collaboration is a mutual recognition process, but you have to provide structure and encouragement to make it happen.

The Many Forms of Recognition

The concept of *cooperation* suggests two or more parties working together for a common purpose. In a practical way, it's a form of *mutual recognition* where people choose to recognize one another for a variety of reasons:

- One party has something the other wants.
- The parties can't meet their objective without working together.
- The parties like and respect one another.
- Something "bad" will happen to one, both, or all parties if they don't cooperate.
- The parties recognize one another as having value— ideas, resources, influence.

Think about examples of people cooperating on a task or project. What generally comes to mind is people from different areas of responsibility coming together as "partners" for some specified period of time until the work is done. Neither person has responsibility for the other, yet both have *accountability* to a client or customer and *responsibility* for getting the work done according to some set standards.

Making It Their Business

The manager of a large utility had instructed field employees to return borrowed tools to the shop for storing and reissuing, as needed. Instead, tools were being left in trucks or general work areas without being returned. Frustrated, he called everyone together. "I'm not tracking down missing tools and equipment anymore. If you've a problem with missing tools, figure it out among yourselves. I'm here to help you, not clean up after you." From then on, the employees resolved such problems on their own. And, rather than *berate* them, the manager got to *congratulate* them on their resourcefulness.

It should be the same way with you and your employees. The more you're able to get your employees to recognize their relationship with you and one another as one of "co-operating" ("operating together"), the better the outcome will be for you, your employees, and your customers.

Cooperating is a way of establishing constructive relationships and generating productive outcomes. In cooperative ventures people can give constructive feedback to one another without having it construed negatively. And, when things are going well, they get to compliment one another by giving encouragement and positive reinforcement.

And, when it comes to recognition, positive reinforcement is certainly preferable to negative attention. No one really enjoys playing "critical parent"—especially if you're a manager with a full plate of responsibilities. Who has the time to be holding hands, anyway? And, it's not much fun getting criticized, either—as we all know. Positive reinforcement is a process of *recognizing* employees doing things right just as much as *catching* them doing the right things. Because savvy managers know that employees perform better in situations where morale is high, they design work projects and assign job responsibilities in ways that enable employees to be successful.

To facilitate cooperation in the workplace, smart managers:

- Create "win-win" situations where all parties see the benefit of working together.
- Establish "co-operating" as a required way of working.
- Set goals that are realistic and, therefore, achievable.

> **Key Term**
>
> **Recognizing** Expressing appreciation of someone's efforts, a positive experience for both parties. The meaning of "recognizing" comes from the Latin verb *cognoscere*—to "know" or to "see"—and *re*, "again." So, to recognize someone means we identify or see the person based on characteristics or attributes that are familiar in us. We "recall" these factors and are able to identify the person because of what they trigger within us. Their actions are familiar. In the workplace, seeing, knowing, or recognizing a person—again and again—is the repetitive process of expressing appreciation. It's usually meant as a positive gesture and helps reinforce positive behaviors.

- Begin with short assignments that can be performed quickly and successfully—to boost confidence and build skills for more difficult assignments.
- Recognize the abilities of their employees and encourage them to use one another's talents.
- Express appreciation when employees work in "co-operative" ways.

Cooperation enables everyone to achieve together what they could not independently.

Communication

As we discussed in Chapter 3, communication is a powerful means of recognizing employees—just as silence can be an extremely hurtful way of punishing employees. Of course, the process of communication doesn't happen by merely wishing it so. You've got to make it happen.

In this day of voice mail, e-mail, faxes, cellular phones, pagers, satellite links, closed-circuit TV—you name it!—there is no excuse for failing to communicate.

Perhaps one of the best examples of effective communication came in the heat of a union-organizing campaign. Organizers for the union were fomenting employee dissatisfaction over their employer's pay program. They promised union wage scales would bring employees more money and better benefits if they'd support the union by voting it in. Rising to

Keep It Simple, Supervisor (KISS)
Prompted by a process called "Work Out"—taking time and money out of workplace processes by taking "work" out— global giant GE pulled the plug some time ago on fancy reports, slick presentations, and mountains of memos. The company compels employees to "talk to one another." "We communicate the old fashioned way— you know?—by picking up the phone and talking things out," according to one GE employee. "No more CYAWP—cover your you-know-what with paper! We don't have time for that, and it sure demands a level of trust that memos could never bring about."

the challenge, company management mounted a full-scale campaign of its own to educate employees over pay issues. The company explained how the pay system was structured— with pay ranges and salary grades benchmarked to comparable jobs in the marketplace. They published pay and benefits information about the union's contracts with other companies. They compared the income for union employees with employee income under the company's plan. They were able to demonstrate that employee compensation under the company's program was better than that for like jobs under the union's contracts. They made a similar case for benefits. In the end, management was able to convince employees of the value and competitiveness of its current program.

Unfortunately, the company had not done a good job in communicating anything about the pay system before the campaign. It took a union-organizing effort to get the company to do what it should have been doing all along. The union campaign forced management to adopt a program of ongoing communication around its pay and benefits plans. A comparison of the results of employee opinion surveys taken before union-organizing efforts began and following the campaign revealed a significant improvement in employee satisfaction over pay and benefits. Ironically, the company had made no changes in its plans—management had just simply and effectively communicated!

Another means of communicating effectively about benefits is to provide each employee annually with a personalized statement showing the value of his or her benefits in specific

Two-Way Communication

Employee opinion surveys are an effective means of fostering two-way communication on larger issues affecting employee morale. By soliciting employee feedback on a range of subjects—from pay to supervision, from training to equal opportunity—managers can "listen" to employee concerns in a nonthreatening way, using both quantitative and anecdotal survey techniques. With data in hand, managers can discuss employee concerns in an informed way and work to address areas of need or misunderstanding. Two-way communication is another example of saying to employees that you *recognize* the worth and value of what they have to say and that you want to work with them.

dollar amounts. Employees often fail to understand the full value of their total compensation program, which includes not only direct but also indirect pay—like Social Security taxes, paid time off, unemployment taxes, and employer-paid benefits and subsidies. It all adds up! And communicating effectively helps employees better understand how they are being recognized and rewarded. If your company does not provide such information, talk to someone in your organization—a human resources or finance manager—and get the information for your employees. Alternatively, either you or a company representative could present the information at a meeting of your employees or in a roundtable discussion, using visuals or handouts to show the typical benefits for all or selected income levels. However you do it, just do it!

Savvy managers understand the importance of communicating on such issues. It's a double form of recognition: first, it's recognizing employees as important and deserving of your time to communicate the "business" of their personal financial relationship with your organization, and second, it's identifying the value of the reward system used to recognize their contributions to the organization.

Personal Development

Personal and professional development are important to everyone in the new workplace. Free agent/employees expect to learn new skills and competencies and have access to new

> ### What Are You Hiding?   ⚠ CAUTION! ⚠
> It used to be employees were forbidden to talk about pay. The reason, of course, was that management didn't want to have to deal with unhappy employees or demands for more money. Enlightened managers realize that such edicts only foster distrust on the part of employees: "The pay must be pretty bad or inequitable if no one wants to talk about it." Good, bad, or indifferent, the pay program for your organization is what it is. Everyone should know how it works. Secrecy buys nothing but misunderstanding and mistrust!

knowledge areas to increase their own value to an organization and in the marketplace. It's part of their total reward program. And although employees should be responsible for their own development, smart managers know they have an obligation to provide opportunities and assignments that will enhance personal and professional growth.

There are many ways in which you, as a manager, can facilitate that process:

- Assign job responsibilities and work assignments that are developmental—adjusting to match the skills, interests, and abilities of the individuals involved.
- Use performance planning and, especially, performance evaluation periods to uncover areas requiring further personal and professional development.
- Provide access to company workshops and training programs and allow time for employees to participate. Remember: if you're not continually developing your people, you and they run the risk of becoming "stale," "outdated," and irrelevant together.
- Encourage continued learning outside the work environment. For some new entrants to the workplace, lifelong learning is already a given.
- Build "learning" into your routine as a manager. Talk about the latest developments in your field, business, industry. Monitor what's "hot" and what's not.
- Develop multiple ways to transfer knowledge. Classroom training by itself won't cut it any more. Learner-centered

processes and customized learning experiences are in.

- Provide opportunities for your employees to check out the competition or meet with customers or dialogue with people in other organizations who have information that they can use.
- If your organization has a tuition reimbursement program for enrolling in formal programs of study, encourage your employees to participate.

Think of personal and professional development as an investment in your people and in your future success overall. Smart managers wouldn't dream of operating with outdated equipment or first-generation technology. In today's environment, that would be suicide. Similarly, they couldn't imagine leading a team that was unskilled, unprepared, and ill-equipped to compete in a global economy. Employee development is good business—and, just like other reward and recognition programs, it's part of a total package.

Performance Feedback

For many organizations, reviews of employee performance occur at least annually, if not semiannually. And, all too often, discussions of any adjustments in pay are made part of the performance evaluation process. Understandably, whatever a manager has to say about an employee's performance at that time virtually goes in one ear and out the other as the

For Example

Learning, Information, and Getting Wired
Toyota Motor Manufacturing allocates dedicated space on plant floors for learning. Team members wanting to advance to successive levels of responsibility spend personal time in the learning areas reading and otherwise accessing information that will make them more competent, more knowledgeable, and ready for new responsibilities. Ford Motor announced at the start of the new millennium that it would offer every employee in its 350,000-member workforce a high-speed desktop computer, color printer, and unlimited Internet access to get the company "hardwired" for business. At Ford, communication and learning are serious business.

employee sits quietly waiting to hear the "bottom line," i.e., "How much more money am I going to get?" The value of any constructive comments on how to improve performance is lost.

Even though linking pay with performance is desirable, when an announcement of salary adjustments is linked with discussing performance, the process becomes problematic for both manager and employee. Frequently, the manager ends up writing the performance review in a manner to support what he or she intends to give—or not give—as an adjustment. And, the employee focuses on the reward rather than performance improvement.

Like our school example in Chapter 2, where smiley faces and stars distract from the process of learning, so too discussions about pay during performance evaluation sessions distract from the process of improving performance. No wonder W. Edwards Deming and others have recommended throwing out performance reviews! In many organizations today, performance reviews are unproductive at best and quite often even counterproductive.

If pay-for-performance systems are designed properly, employees will receive rewards according to their investment of performance. How the pay system works will be evident and little or no explanation will be required on the part of the manager. That being the case, managers should be free to concentrate on where they can add value, namely, in coaching employees and in removing obstacles to performance excellence.

> ### Uncoupling the Process
>
> Planning, performing, progress reporting, paying, re-planning, re-forming, performing, reporting, re-paying, etc.—all are like cars in train. Each is a discrete part of a total process. But all the cars of a train don't have to arrive at the same destination at the same time; the cars can be uncoupled and dropped at designated stations along the way. Likewise, you don't need to do all steps in the process at the same time. By uncoupling pay announcements from discussions of performance, managers are able to focus on what it's all about—*performance* and *performance improvement*.

Smart managers use performance feedback to:

- Recognize, not criticize.
- Express appreciation.
- Evaluate strengths and weaknesses.
- Identify developmental opportunities.
- Check for problems—materials, equipment, information, etc.
- Probe for new areas of interest.
- Determine personal and professional goals.
- Offer encouragement.
- Ask how they can be better resources.
- Partner, not preach.

Performance feedback should be a form of ongoing communication and recognition—one that is productive, not punishing, constructive, not manipulative, and timely.

Smart Managing

Constructive Coaching

Ever watch a sporting event where the coach is on the sidelines yelling at the players and criticizing every move? Chances are the team didn't do very well or, if it did, the players weren't particularly joyful. Contrast that picture with one of a coach strategizing with players, putting a hand on a shoulder, applauding their progress. In the first scenario, winning is everything—even at the cost of player esteem. In the second, it's all about building confidence—winning is an outcome of improving performance. Savvy managers use performance feedback as a tool for constructive coaching.

Doing What's Natural

Recognizing employees at work will have to be second nature to managers in the new workplace. Many new employees will be people who were born in the late '70s, '80s, and early '90s raised in the Information Age—the so-called "Net Kids." According to Don Tapscott, author of *Growing up Digital: The Rise of the Net Generation* (New York: McGraw-Hill, 1998), this will be the first time in history when young people will be an authority on something vital to the marketplace, namely, *technology*. Managers will be challenged to keep them motivated and involved. They know all about people like Bill Gates, Steve

Jobs, and Michael Dell, and they're motivated to create wealth for the organization and for themselves. Add these new entrants to the mix of boomers, Generation Xers, Generation Y, and free agent/employees, and you have one *very* interesting scenario, to say the least. Clearly, recognizing employees will require something more than a "one size fits all" approach.

So what's a manager to do? Well, smart managers are adapting their style and their ways of recognizing employees according to the situation and the individuals involved. Understanding their "customers," i.e., their employees, is vitally important. Smart managers know they have to trust their employees' capabilities more and respect them as "free agents." They're designing work assignments and jobs, as we've discussed earlier, to capitalize on the strengths, interests, and talents of these precious resources. Rather than opposing the "natural order" of things and beating down self-esteem, managers of the new workplace are building for the future.

> **Key Term**
>
> **The Net Generation**
> People born between 1977 and 1997, the "techno-crats" of the new workplace. Many in their late teens have run or are running businesses on the Internet. Some are even making "serious money." They've been raised with a global vision; they're educated, innovative, collaborative, flexible, and fast-paced. Add to this the experience we referenced in Chapter 1 of graduating from educational institutions where conflict and violence are a reality, and you've got one set of pretty independent, constantly questioning, highly sophisticated workers.

Savvy managers:

- Accommodate individual differences by knowing their employees better.
- Assess workplace needs and placing the right people with the right talent in the right assignments.
- Consult with employees about program design—Are these the right rewards? Is this the best form of recognition?
- Provide choices so more employees can find the "pathways" that make the most sense.

Building Natural Paths

A landscape architect observed there are two ways to approach laying pathways for a school campus: "One is to lay paths on day one. Be prepared to post signs telling students to 'keep off the grass' when they wander. You may have to put up fences, too. In the end students make their way according to what makes the most sense. Alternatively, you can lay a few paths and let footprints show you where to lay the rest. That way you save a lot of cement and look a lot smarter to your travelers."

- Trust employees to want to do meaningful work and then structuring opportunities to meet their interests.
- Monitor how they themselves are coming across as managers and adjusting their style to be more effective.

Change feels different, and that's natural. Savvy managers are letting go of any preconceptions they've had about empirical models of leading. Instead, they are becoming situational managers by recognizing differences and accommodating needs—just as they would with the ultimate customers for whom their business products and services are intended. They're listening to their employees and letting them suggest how they want to be valued, recognized, and rewarded.

To replicate success, managers must recognize successful behavior. Modeling organizational performance after top performers has long been a way of building performance and teaching others how to be more effective. For generations, efficiency experts, consultants (both internal and external), advisors, and management gurus have followed workers around, observing and measuring their every move. Patterns of behavior of the most efficient were modeled for others to follow. The good news was it gave employees, in general, a better understanding of how to avoid performance pitfalls and cash in on improved performance. The bad news was it was time-consuming, costly, and devaluing of human initiative in that the approach was a "top-down," "outside-in" sort of process. The so-called "experts" in this model of performance improvement were "outsiders" to the process. The experts internal to the process were left out of the design process.

In the new workplace, replicating success depends on those who are "insiders" to the process to develop improvements and evolve even more successful systems of performance. The experts are those who live the experience and are closest to the customer—the point of decision making. Smart managers, therefore, watch for these improvements and recognize the right initiatives when they're exhibited, applaud the successes when they occur, and encourage ongoing invention and innovation.

Savvy managers take responsibility for setting direction and calling the shots. They may not always be right, but they listen to their people, recognize their contributions, and adjust the course of business with feedback from their employees. Savvy managers know when they have to be directive, prescriptive, collaborative, and deferential. They do what's appropriate, what's natural for the circumstances. Their approach is situational and "custom-designed" rather than "one size fits all."

>
>
> **When You're Dancing with Bears**
>
> "When you're dancing with bears," goes a familiar saw, "there's no time to rest." Today's finish to that might well be "...there's no turning back." Founders Steve Jobs and Steve Wozniak built a unique culture at Apple. The design team for Macintosh worked in a separate building marked by a pirate flag on top. Employees believed they were changing the world. Life events and business accomplishments were celebrated. But when successor CEO John Scully cut 20% of the force, the effects were devastating. Apple lost critical talent and it was almost unable to recover.

Enhancing Self-Worth

Enlightened managers understand that today's free agent/ employees are in business for themselves. Cliff Hakim, author of *We Are All Self-Employed: The New Social Contract for Working in a Changed World* (San Francisco: Berrett-Koehler Publishers, 1994), was among the first of leading-edge thinkers to advance the belief that the biggest mistake workers in the new workplace can make is to think they are working for someone else.

Building Self-Worth

Smart managers recognize that employees who are building self-worth are:

- Embarking upon a process of self-change
- Replacing fears—such as job loss—with a passion for their work
- Acting independently—by expressing their authenticity—and interdependently—by choosing to collaborate with others
- Approaching work and work relationships based on *equality*—"I'm not 'subordinate'"—and *competence*—"I have worth"
- Viewing their career as a lifetime endeavor
- Working with the belief that the world offers what they need and that they can make a difference

paraphrased from *We Are All Self-Employed*, p. 20

Smart Managing

Professor Rosabeth Moss Kanter of the Harvard Business School is another leading-edge thinker to point out in the early 1980s—even before Hakim and others—that what employees were coming to expect and wanted most was "employability security," namely, the ability to get a job easily because of the knowledge and skills acquired in their current positions. Savvy managers were advised at that time to help employees build competencies that would make them want to stay with their current employers because of the value of their learning experience. Consequently, in the new workplace, savvy managers are concentrating even more deliberately on recognizing opportunities that will enable their employees to build *self-worth*. Indeed, employees and managers alike are coming to recognize that *enhanced self-worth* is the *new-age currency* in a global marketplace.

Of course, increased self-worth implies increased earnings opportunity. No one wants to be taken for granted, and employees who are inappropriately paid will likely market their skills to the next bidder. Smart managers, therefore, balance skill enhancement and increased self-worth with appropriate recognition and rewards.

But not everything translates into cash. Just like our "turkey" story in Chapter 2, cash awards have no lasting value. Eventually, they have to be replaced by bigger and bigger awards. In fact, many companies in the U.S. have been eliminating "Christmas bonuses" because of their irrelevance to business performance and questionable value to employees. Recognition, on the other hand, has trophy appeal—if it's done right—and the value has lasting effect over time.

Smart managers also realize that *self*-recognition is its own reward! When employees recognize their own efforts and successes, that self-recognition is critical to their building self-esteem and appreciating their self-worth.

> **Same Old Same Old**
>
> "If you always do what you've always done, you'll always get what you always got." This expression has held true for many generations. A better version for the new workplace might be "If you always do what you've always done, you'll be gone—forever!!"
>
> Concentrate on staying current as a manager. Read. Continuously learn. Don't undervalue employees, younger or older. Seek new ideas. Try different suggestions. Embrace change. Model flexibility. Be open to mistakes—even your own. And learn from those you steward. Even from your youngest will come pearls of wisdom.

The challenge for managers in the new workplace will be how to adapt to employees who have differing levels of self-worth and varying expectations. For example, the youngest entrants to the new workplace often have high self-esteem and even higher expectations of accumulating wealth. Smart managers will need to recognize the independent nature of these employees and capitalize on their natural inclination to collaborate and network with others. Managers will also have to place more emphasis on the accomplishments of the team. That's not to say individual recognition won't be important. It will. But the Net generation of workers will be starting out from a different place with respect to self-esteem. Compliments *per se* will not be where they're at, but rather "Show me the money," i.e., the challenge, the opportunity, the new project, the next discovery, *and* the money! Savvy managers will need patience, flexibility, and an enlightened appreciation of the "currency" of self-worth.

Leading in the new workplace will require patience and commitment, among other attributes. Smart managers will be:

- Architects of connectivity
- Facilitators of information acquisition
- Agents of discovery
- Designers of change
- Acquirers of talent
- Brokers of knowledge
- Mentors of collaboration and teamwork

Increasing Competence

The concept of "intellectual capital" has been around for some time, and its importance is increasing dramatically. Accountants have grappled with the challenge of calculating "goodwill" as a factor of valuation when assessing the market value of a business or other legal entity. Intellectual capital is the new frontier for accountancy thinking and number crunching. Investors have their own way of assessing intellectual capital, judging from the market multiples for technology and Internet companies traded on the exchanges, many of which either are unprofitable or generate profits lower than those of industrial counterparts.

And, in the battle for marketplace dominance in computing and information technology, intellectual capital is at the heart of legal conflicts between Microsoft and the government, between telecommunications giants and long-distance carriers, the Defense Department and foreign countries, and scores of other competitors and predators in a global economy.

In the new workplace, managers are now stewards of "knowledge workers" and skill-based performance systems. Reward and recognition programs that were once oriented to the least com-

> **Intellectual capital** The knowledge, mental competencies, ideas, and insights of your employees, as well as the trade secrets, experiences, and best practices of the organization. According to Tom Brown, editor of the MG "New Ideas" Web site, @mgeneral.com, "You're probably doing a poor job of capitalizing on your company's intellect if you can't hear the 'cha-ching' of workers and managers thinking their way to success right now"
> Source: "Ringing Up Intellectual Capital," *Management Review,* January 1998.

mon denominator—minimum starting rates, bonus thresholds, medians, midpoints, bell curves, pay targets, average wage increases—are only now beginning to focus on skills, competence, knowledge, and, yes, intellectual capital. And there's a long way to go before pay systems catch up with the challenge of recognizing and rewarding intellectual capital. In the meantime, the onus is on you as a manager to retain, develop, and leverage the intelligence of your team.

Smart managers are recognizing intellectual capital in every size, shape, and configuration imaginable:

- Knowledge of software systems and related applications
- Abilities relating to producing goods and services
- Relationships with key human resources and other key stakeholders
- Interpersonal skills and skills relating to teamwork
- Knowledge of processes, products, and services
- Problem-solving abilities
- Special knowledge that would be difficult to recover if you lost the employee(s)
- Insight into the market and how best to convert opportunities into sales
- Knowledge of competitors and how to beat them
- Knowledge and abilities to bring new products to market "just in time"

Every one of these examples represents opportunity for smart managers to recognize and reward employees for the right stuff.

An additional part of intellectual capital is as something only recently investigated by psychologists and not yet full appreciated by many managers—"emotional intelligence." This term has been defined and used in various ways, but John D. Mayer and Peter Salovey, who were first to define the term, gave the following definition in 1997: "Emotional intelligence involves the ability to perceive accurately, appraise, and express emotion; the ability to access and/or generate feelings when they facilitate thought; the ability to understand emotion and emotional knowledge; and the ability to regulate emotions to promote emotional and intellectual growth."*

Smart managers know that these are important abilities that they should recognize in their employees, to ensure that the employees who exhibit them see that their talents are valued. And, recognizing them publicly ensures that others understand what standards are expected as they work to develop such skills.

Key Term
Emotional intelligence The ability to perceive accurately, appraise, and express emotion; the ability to access and/or generate feelings when they facilitate thought; the ability to understand emotion and emotional knowledge; and the ability to regulate emotions to promote emotional and intellectual growth.

Informal Recognition

Just as important as knowing *what* to recognize is knowing *when*, *where*, and *how* to recognize employees who are exhibiting the *what*. Moreover, the array of recognition options and the types of rewards range from *no cost* and *low cost* to *high cost* and *"far-out,"* from *superficial* to *substantive*, and from *informal* to *formal*. And, although we've cited already a number of examples of both recognition processes and rewards, we need to take a closer look at the general classifications of recognition.

Bob Nelson, author of *1001 Ways to Reward Employees* (New York: Workman Publishing, 1994), says, "Few management concepts are as solidly founded as the idea that positive reinforcement—rewarding behavior you want repeated—works." More than ever, in a world of downsizing, doing more with less, and constant change, recognition and reward are vitally important to morale and creating goodwill between employees and managers. Smart managers know that employees are not captives. To retain and develop competent and caring workers, they need to express appreciation in meaningful ways. Recognition needs to be consistent, frequent, and part of the organizational

*"What Is Emotional Intelligence?" in *Emotional Intelligence and Emotional Development*, edited by Peter Salovey and David J. Sluyter (New York: Basic Books, 1997) p. 10.

Building Trust for Better Business
American Express Financial Advisors found an important difference between its financial advisors who stuck with facts and figures when selling prospects and its advisors who were savvy to the emotional reactions of clients. The latter group of advisors were able to suggest how they would work as partners with their clients to ensure good communication, understanding, and trust. Based on its findings, the company developed a competency model covering key areas of emotional intelligence. It trained some 60 advisors and found that their results far exceeded those of advisors not trained in these skills. Learning what emotions drive client decisions pays off.
Source: Scott Hays, "American Express Taps into the Power of Emotional Intelligence," *Workforce*, July 1999.

fabric. And, here too, one size does not fit all. Informal recognition is an individual thing, up to the manager, while formal recognition tends to be more of an organizational arrangement.

Examples of informal recognition include:

- Time off with pay
- Lunch "on the house"
- Cards and letters for all occasions
- Certificates and commemorative memorabilia of all types—for outstanding service, better solutions, top productivity, etc.
- An ongoing award named in honor of an outstanding employee
- News articles and cameos about people who make it happen
- Flowers, candy, food, small gifts—anything that says, "You're special!"

Informal recognition Random, unexpected acts of appreciation, ways that a manager acknowledges employee efforts or accomplishments as he or she becomes aware of them.
Oftentimes, they are simple comments: "Thank you" or "Wow! That's great!" or "What a terrific idea!" Or recognition may take the form of tickets for two to a show, a letter of appreciation to the employee with a copy to the head of the company, or a gift certificate to a popular store or restaurant. Awards, if any, are "re-earnable" and are not intended necessarily to be an "entitlement" for ongoing performance.

Smart Managing

Be Authentic

Avoid trivializing employee contributions. If your way of recognizing employees is "fake," insincere, or slapdash, you're likely to do more harm than good. Get to know your employees. Observe their successes. Listen for their likes and dislikes—it's a little like waiting for hints about what someone wants for a birthday. Personalize the recognition. Deliver the compliment with sincerity and genuine appreciation. And yes, it's OK to have fun; in fact, it's generally very appropriate—as long as the fun is in good taste and not at anyone's expense.

- Special "timeouts" with fun and refreshments
- Balloons, penguins, and other fun stuff

Whatever you do, make it *appropriate*, *timely*, and *public*! But above all, avoid encouraging competition among employees, departments, or work units. Any competition should be directed externally, not focused internally. The idea is to bring people together in celebration of their uniqueness—their special events, contributions, and talents—not to divide them. It's all about one team, one family, one organization, one great bunch of people!

Formal Recognition

Formal recognition tends to be about things "organizational"— achievement of organizational objectives, meeting and beating performance goals, solving departmental or organizational problems. Formal recognition programs tend to link people together—the emphasis is on team results, group performance, organizational success. Formal celebration is often on a grander scale than informal recognition, with significant dollars involved. And the criteria for recognition are fairly standardized, to ensure consistency across organizational boundaries. Compared with informal recognition, formal recognition programs tend to:

- Look out over longer time horizons
- Incorporate benchmarks, e.g., service achievements, profit objectives, etc.
- Be performance-based

- Focus on the creation of value for the organization, e.g., employee commitment, market appreciation, investor loyalty, etc.
- Be connected with compensation programs
- Involve both *reward* (now you see it) and *risk* (now you don't)
- Be scheduled, rather than spontaneous

Formal recognition programs usually require top management approval. Examples of such programs are gainsharing, profit sharing, short- and long-term incentive programs, and stock and stock option programs. It's not always possible—or advisable—for individual managers to implement such programs on their own. But smart managers know the importance of measuring performance and recognizing the critical success factors that drive their business. By being "in the know," they're better able to assist in the design of any major program.

If you're in a situation where a large-system reward program is being designed, here are some suggestions:

- Advocate for broad participation: involve as many people as possible in designing the program.
- Emphasize team-based plans, to recognize collaboration and synergy.
- Get involved in setting the objectives.
- Involve your people to the greatest extent possible. At a minimum, get their input.

Encourage full disclosure of the objectives of the program, as well as the intent behind it and what it purports to measure and reward, so all employees understand how the plan works and how best to achieve both outcomes and recognition.

If the current programs are not addressing the needs of your people and supporting the work you're trying to accomplish, suggest ways in which they can be improved. And if your organization doesn't have formal recognition programs, suggest setting up such programs. We'll take a closer look at a number of plans in Chapter 10.

> ## Up, Up, Away
> Following the sale of its business, management set aside certain proceeds for longer-term employees as an incentive to continue under new ownership for some specified period of time, after which each would receive a payout. Rather than leave the reserve "in some sleepy bank account," management determined to add an element of employee control—direction into any number of investment instruments. Investment of the reserve resulted in an impressive return, which allowed management to accelerate the payouts.

If you're in a situation where you have more latitude to design your own formal programs, consider designs that:

- Increase teamwork and synergy
- Recognize groups
- Reward teams for project work and desired results
- Build group knowledge, skills, and abilities
- Have cross-functional appeal by involving support personnel as well as employees who may be closer to the "action"
- Enhance organizational pride
- Align your people with the goals of the organization

Confer with experts in the field of compensation and reward systems to ensure you've got the right approach to compensation, one that includes elements of recognition and reward that builds higher levels of performance. And focus on a "win-win" strategy for building organizational value while enhancing earning potential for your employees.

Formal recognition programs require communication, feedback, support, and total understanding. Savvy managers understand that the most important role they play in large-system reward programs is that of communicator and coach.

Celebrating Outcomes

If all you did as a manager was to "pay compliments" and "pay out rewards," you'd being doing only half the job—and you could expect just about half the return on your "investment"—at best! Part of the value in recognizing and rewarding an *individ-*

ual or a *team* lies in the overall effect it has on others and the workplace as a whole.

Whether it's a seller's market, where employees can change jobs readily, or a buyer's market, where employees are potentially locked in, nothing is more exhilarating than the feeling of success and the accompanying recognition that goes along with it. Yes, enthusiasm is contagious. And, success does tend to breed success. But *recognition* and *celebration* are essential tools for attracting, developing, and retaining envied resources *and* for encouraging continued success. The *art* of celebration lies in your ability as a manager to influence others to join in the fun and to visualize themselves in the center of the next success story.

Savvy managers go to extreme lengths to showcase each and every employee at one time or another—individually, in groups, in private, in public, in the limelight, in the media, formally, informally—any and every way they can. Savvy managers also make work fun! By using a variety of approaches and different types of rewards, they're able to make things interesting, entertaining, personal, and, above all else, meaningful.

Organizations that understand the value of recognition have come to appreciate that the *art of recognition* is a form of *intellectual* capital. These are acquired skills and, as such, can be learned. Companies and managers who are most proficient in the art of recognition have made recognition a way of life, a value of their cultural system, and a competitive weapon against all others who would dare to rob them of their precious resources—their people. Among the outstanding corporate performers in this arena is Disneyland in Anaheim, California. Their superstar members are celebrated and immortalized by having their names painted on one of the Main Street windows and they receive a replica of the window to commemorate the event during a formal celebration.

Celebrating employees' "gifts" is important—not only for those who serve in today's highly complex and often impersonal workplace but also for those who follow. It's a manager's way of saying, "I know you could have chosen to work for other managers or organizations. Thanks for choosing us."

Manager's Checklist for Chapter 7

❏ Design various ways to foster mutual recognition by getting employees to "co-operate" more as partners than as individual contributors.

❏ Appreciate the value of communication as a supreme form of recognition and an enhancement of the reward system.

❏ Understand how personal development and performance feedback contribute to the reward and recognition process.

❏ Competence and learning are "new age" forms of currency. Smart managers understand how valuable they are to employees and to organizations.

❏ Whether formal or informal, recognition and rewards must be celebrated to be of maximum benefit to all.

Understanding How Rewards Work

The business of rewards is big business! Compensation experts ply their trade with scientific precision, conversing in a language of compensable factors, quartiles, re-earnable incentives, long- and short-term bonus plans, referral incentives, lines of sight, sign-on bonuses, tin parachutes, golden handcuffs, and retention incentive plans. Like the flavor of the month or the plan for the moment, rewards are in! Bringing everyone "up to speed"—at least to the level of top performers, if not beyond—requires incentives and lots of them! The elixir for all that ails an organization—be it poor production, employee turnover, or chronic absenteeism—is just one magical blend of incentives away. And joining the armies of systems experts, compensation analysts, and reward mavens are legions of award and recognition vendors hawking everything from pins, plaques, and pens to exotic cruises, gift catalogues, and lifestyle experiences. Yes, indeed, the business of rewards is BIG business!!

So what's wrong with a little hype? Nothing! Absolutely nothing!! But, it raises a legitimate question: Why all the emphasis on incentives, recognition, and rewards? Are we becoming a

nation hooked on incentives? How is it that countries like
Germany, Japan, and Sweden produce quality goods and services without all the incentives and elaborate schemes of carrots
and sticks? What drives our seemingly insatiable fascination
with rewards and reward systems?

As we indicated at the start of our journey in Chapter 2,
strong proponents of incentives argue that pay is a motivator:
identify the right behaviors, dangle the right come-on, step on
the right pedal, and people will jump through hoops to perform
the right tricks in pursuit of the metaphorical brass ring. The
underlying assumption—predicated on a theory of stimulus and
response—suggests that people will behave like trained seals
and perform on command to win rewards. And, in fact, there
are some who will respond accordingly—up to a point. Others
may not. Alfie Kohn refers to this belief system as "pop behav-
iorism" (*Punished by Rewards*, p. 120).

Opponents of the use of incentives argue that they are
demeaning and manipulative, they distract employees from the
importance of their work, and they divide employees by encouraging internal competition and political pettiness.

As we observed earlier, on whichever side of the issue you
stand, everyone seems to agree, either explicitly or implicitly,
that incentives influence behavior in the short term. But their
effectiveness on long-term results is questionable at best and, at
worst, devastating.

⚠ CAUTION! ⚠

Watch What You're Saying— Explicitly and Implicitly!

Incentives carry *explicit* and *implicit* messages. One
employer implemented an incentive plan to compensate employees for
referrals leading to hires. When asked about the program, an employee
responded, "Some days they can't pay me enough to stay here. Fees
help buy my silence on what it's really like—at least until the new guy
gets through the door." Another split her fees with the prople she
brought in through referrals. "Frankly, I'd feel guilty once they learned
what it's like here, if I hadn't given them something," she said.

If we probe a little deeper, we find there is a link between this penchant for rewards and our economic system for marketing to customers.

Think about it! We sell consumers on the idea of needing a particular product, usually based on lifestyle wants. "It makes life easier." "You can retire early." "You'll be on easy street." "It performs tasks in half the time, so you benefit by having more time to do other things." To sell customers on what we want them to buy, we "un-sell" them on their present situation. Indeed, we may even sow a few seeds of discontent, so they become unhappy with what they have or, better still, don't have—especially if base pay is low. Or maybe we suggest they *deserve* a "piece of the action"—which implies they're entitled to their "cut." And, to up the ante, we influence their view of where they could be by depicting how *others* are better off—principally, because others have something they should want. "This is the most *popular* model." "*Discriminating consumers* choose brand X over brand Y." "You deserve the *finer* things life has to offer." We get people to visualize how they could be happier or reach some personal level of satisfaction by having what others already have. Call it envy or call it greed, it's a model of "wanting" based on some principle of *deprivation* and *dissatisfaction.*

Putting it all together, if we as managers believe people are not motivated, i.e., lazy, and need a little jump-start to get going, and then we integrate some reward system based on the cultivation of *envy* or *want*—"They'll have it easier because they can earn more money" or "They will have it better if they recruit others to share the workload," we end up with a slick system of "carrots" (a better way of life) and "sticks" (unhappiness with present conditions, or the threat of performance warnings, or the fear of job loss, or whatever). In the end, the model we've just described is one based on *distrust, fear,* and *envy:*

- *Distrust*—I can't trust my employees to do the right stuff on their own.
- *Fear*—I have to intervene or it won't happen; I could even get fired as a manager if I don't get my employees to perform.

- *Envy*—I'll motivate my employees by selling them on how much better their life will be with more money or how much more popular they'll become with this or that reward or recognition.

It's an interesting picture, but how does that reflect on us as managers? Well, in a way, it's like looking in a mirror. How about *distrustful*, *fearful*, and *greedy*? After all, I must lust after what others have, if I assume my employees are driven by the same desires. It also makes us appear *manipulative*. Such attributes serve only to distance managers from their employees and erode any feelings of trust—a key attribute for effective managers, as we discussed in Chapter 3.

If this is a reflection that doesn't disturb you, if you're OK with what you see, then join the throng to "motivate" the masses. If, on the other hand, your response is "Pretty harsh picture" or "Something must be wrong" or "That isn't who I am," then read further. Even if you find this thought only somewhat accurate, then consider an alternative image of a manager who is *trusting, empowering*, and *generous*:

- *Trusting*—I trust my employees to make good decisions, and I am available to them as a resource, collaborator, and partner.
- *Empowering*—I work with my people to remove obstacles to their success. We're working together to build a reputation we can be proud of.
- *Generous*—I pay people fairly and competitively. If other employers pay incentives to their employees, I will consider matching their program or provide an alternative approach to retain my employees by protecting their overall earnings potential.

This second picture does not preclude paying incentives. And it certainly does not exclude employee recognition—quite the contrary. It avoids any hint of manipulation by placing emphasis first on doing the right stuff. For example, employees should be proud of where they work. They should want others to join their work community, because it's a great place to be.

After all, word of mouth is the best form of advertising. If employees like what they do and where they work, they'll tell others—automatically. Although you may have to spend a little to "get the word out," to get people to come to your place of business, you shouldn't have to break the bank with advertising dollars, so to speak. If you decide to pay hiring bonuses or referral commissions, do it to be competitive with pay practices elsewhere or to be fair or for some other reason, but not because employees need to be manipulated to induce others to come to work with you.

You Get What You Pay for—and Sometimes More

The expression "you get what you pay for" applies to employers as well as customers. If managers don't pay competitively, they probably won't get workers who are more productive and self-motivated. Similarly, if they do pay competitively but don't provide work environments that value and recognize employees or are satisfying to be part of, they probably won't get or retain better workers either. Going one step beyond, without the right philosophy with respect to rewards and recognition and without the right systems, you may inadvertently be "buying" a whole lot more in the way of problems and hidden costs.

Smart managers understand there's a direct correlation between employee commitment and how "generous" ("empowering") or "stingy" managers appear to employees. The following table illustrates this correlation:

> **It Must Not Be Worthwhile**
>
> **CAUTION!**
>
> If every time you have a problem with employees you throw money at it, i.e., an incentive, employees may conclude that anything you're not willing to pay an incentive for must not be worth doing. Before paying incentives, consider factors of equipment, environment, training, personal motives, and supervisory support. Otherwise, you may be wasting money and overlooking the source of the problem. Worse yet, you may be sending messages that take away any natural incentive for employees to tackle other problems unless bribed.

If managers provide or allow minimal	Employees will provide or show minimal
• Pay	• Output—How can I get away with doing the least?
• Recognition	• Regard—Why should I care about this place?
• Employee involvement	• Input of ideas and suggestions for improvement
• Autonomy or freedom to act	• Initiative
• Training	• Expertise
• Positive reinforcement	• Loyalty
• Praise	• Self-esteem
• Opportunity to be a "team"	• Teamwork
• Respect	• Courtesy

Of course, the reverse is also true. If managers are generous, employees feel disposed to do more. If managers provide training, employee expertise will improve. If managers are respectful, employees are courteous in return. And so forth.

There are many examples of managers and companies that have gotten what they paid for—and more. Eastern Airlines "bought" employee discord, strikes, and eventually bankruptcy. Sears Roebuck in California "bought" scrutiny by state consumer protection officials in 1992 over allegedly defrauding customers when it converted employees to commission and reportedly threatened them with job loss or transfer if they didn't meet their quota of car repair sales. The loss of employee commitment and consumer confidence is a steep price to pay for poor management practices and pay schemes portrayed as reward systems.

Before initiating any kind of recognition or reward program, savvy managers ask, "What am I not doing now that I could do to make a significant difference in solving problems or improving results, without using incentives?" They then go about addressing the non-incentive needs before introducing any new program of rewards. By addressing the non-incentive issues, savvy managers know that they are recognizing their employees by meeting their needs. In essence, they *think through* the issues before simply "throwing money" at the problems. By embarking upon a systematic process of analysis and problem

> ## Begin with Results
> Recognizing and rewarding employees is vital. Before instituting any new initiative, smart managers ask if it will:
> * Be aligned with corporate objectives?
> * Be a "win-win" for customers, employees, and other key stakeholders?
> * Be appropriate for the efforts expected?
> * Enhance team relations?
> * Benefit the business and employees in both the short and long term?
> * Build a favorable reputation for all involved?
> * Permit employees to use their discretion, e.g., to avert unseen problems?
> * Provide options for the differing needs and wants of employees?
> * Generate any adverse or undesirable results?

solving, savvy managers avoid the pitfalls of wasting money or provoking "stinkin' thinkin'" on the part of their employees. Inappropriate or excessive use of incentives can prompt employees to conclude:

* "If doing this part of my job is so important as to warrant an incentive, then the rest of my job can't be all that important."
* "If referring someone for employment is a compensable event, then why should I refer anyone unless I'm paid?"
* "That's not my job, but I might do it if they made it worth my while."
* "Why be concerned about perfect attendance, when I don't get a bonus for it?"
* "Where is that in my job description?"

Once the organizational, operational, and personal obstacles have been addressed, managers can focus on implementing a total reward system that integrates individual and organizational, short- and long-term objectives, and explicit and implicit recognition into a performance-based reward system.

Pay for Performance

Beginning with the end in mind invariably brings managers to forge a direct link between pay and performance. And, considering what we know about the potentially adverse impact of short-term incentives on long-term performance, managers who are inclined toward incentives are compelled to consider reward systems that address long-term and short-term concerns, to obviate the risk of a long-term drop-off in performance.

Of course, compensation is only one area affecting organizational performance. We've touched on several others, such as organizational culture, leadership styles, guiding principles, development of people, organizational structure—including team-based designs and communication, such as extensive sharing of information. But, when it comes to compensation, smart managers understand the importance of paying employees well and providing a total reward approach linked to individual and organizational performance. We'll discuss various types of compensation programs in Chapter 10.

Reward programs seek to identify factors employees can be compensated for such as job tasks, performance results, skills, competencies, objectives, and desired outcomes. Moreover, as the workplace changes and organizational structures continue to shift from individual jobs and discrete tasks to teams and process responsibilities, even more emphasis will be placed on *process* factors and *team* results. As a consequence, base compensation programs are moving away from cumbersome pay structures having an infinite number of salary grades, each with a minimum and maximum limit, to "skinnier" structures with a limited number of "bands" having broader pay ranges all in the name

> **Key Term**
>
> **Total reward program** All cash and non-cash components of the reward system, including base pay, bonuses, variable or "re-earnable" pay, as well as benefits, recognition systems, stock options, gainsharing plans, etc. A total reward program is characterized by differing levels of rewards and varying designs according to the employee groups being targeted for recognition and rewards. The program contains different elements relating to short- and long-term objectives, and it is inextricably linked to the strategies and mission of the organization.

of flexibility to accommodate the changing nature of work and employee roles.

Moreover, as noted earlier, employee base pay programs are changing over from fixed or "entitlement" programs to variable and "re-earnable" pay programs, where some component of pay is dependent upon achieving certain performance standards or financial goals. Payouts are not added to employees' base compensation but are treated as discrete, nonrecurring rewards.

Some contend that compensation is the "accelerator" for turning around business enterprises and the key to creating "great companies" (Patricia K. Zingheim and Jay R. Schuster, *Pay People Right,* San Francisco: Jossey-Bass Publishers, 2000). And, certainly, turnaround stories like the one led by Jack Stack of Springfield Remanufacturing Company (SRC) described in Chapter 5 present a compelling case for developing the right compensation system. But you have to look at all the other factors that go into building successful organizations or effecting successful turnarounds.

At SRC it wasn't just compensation. It was also extensive education, relentless communication, bold leadership, intense involvement, mutual respect, vision, commitment, planning, and focus on the long term. Compensation was a management value: pay people appropriately and generously according to the collective success of the enterprise. It was a given. It was a logical calculation based on the financial dimensions of the business. It was the right payout for commitment and dedication.

The same can be said of successful, ongoing ventures as well. It's the whole-company/whole-system approach that pays off. Smart managers understand that pay should be a natural consequence of performance; it does not drive it. Let me repeat: *Pay should be a natural consequence of performance; it does not drive it.* They fully appreciate the importance of rewarding performance, but they focus their attention on designing, building, and managing excellent systems—with the right people, values, goals, measures, and feedback loops to enhance overall performance.

According to Chuck Lindberg, president of C.A.L. Consulting Group, Inc., "Rewards have a tremendous influence when people decide to accept or reject an employment offer. And they can

Ye Olde Lemonade Stand

Workers of Ye Olde Lemonade Stand were hired and assigned jobs as "specialists"—buyers, cutters, de-seeders, squeezers, mixers, pourers, and servers. No one was viewed as an internal customer, and everyone did his or her own thing. Then came the "Process Revolution." Ye Olde was transformed into a magnificent system of process coordinators, each accountable to another for "low seed standards," "high product purity," and "on-time service" to the customer. Pay was predicated on achieving standards, satisfying customers, and teamwork. Process owners (formerly workers) understood the whole system, they were totally rewarded, and it was good!

(adaptation courtesy of C.A.L. Consulting Group, St. Paul, MN)

impact morale negatively, if they are not managed in a way that is perceived as fair by employees." We've certainly seen situations where employees have gone all out, perhaps doubling productivity from a prior period, only to be "rewarded" with the same increase as those producing less. Talk about having a negative impact on morale!

Even more significant, the "implicit employment contract" continues to change, and it is having a definite impact in the area of rewards and recognition. According to Lindberg, "Some software engineers in Silicon Valley have their own agents, just like sports figures might use, to get the best possible compensation package from an employer." Indeed, the "star" system appears alive and well in the marketplace of the future. Moreover, Lindberg adds, "Jobs, as we've known them, are going away. They are being replaced by 'process roles' with the accompanying 'process role descriptions and process role results-based pay.'"

So what are managers to make of all of this? Well, here are several key points:

- Entitlement pay—when employees feel "entitled" to a raise regardless of performance—is going away.
- Linking pay to performance results appears essential for the new workplace.
- Pay must be regarded as a natural outcome of performance, not a driver of it.

- Jobs are changing; therefore, reward systems must change accordingly.
- Employees must be made aware of the economic dimensions of the business and how their roles directly relate.
- Communication and extensive information sharing are vital to employees' overall understanding of how the larger organizational entity is performing.
- Employees should be generously rewarded and regarded as valued stakeholders and partners in progress.
- Long-term incentives must be part of a total mix of rewards to ensure ongoing results.
- Pay options must be flexible.

One last thought, a reminder—not everyone is the same. Different people have different interests and motives. Total reward programs are naturally flexible. They have options, such that employees can choose a non-cash option like extra vacation in lieu of a cash payout or choose to participate in one plan rather than another. In fact, some organizations, such as in the public sector, are restricted as to the amount of compensation and rewards employees can receive. In such cases, other forms of recognition can be adopted to ensure fair and equitable expression of appreciation for the performance contributions of employees.

Understanding Wants and Needs

Not everyone is influenced by money. Depending on where people are in their careers, in their jobs, in their life, individual needs and wants will vary. Yet managers frequently will make assumptions on behalf of their employees that may be totally irrelevant—and that satisfy neither the wants of the individual nor the needs of the organization.

Smart managers involve their employees in the process of designing a total reward program. They learn what's important to them as individuals and as groups. They understand how their employees want to be appreciated, what they need to learn and want to learn, and how aware they are of the overall business.

They understand employees' personal goals and objectives and appreciate their desire to be part of something larger than themselves. Smart managers educate their employees and explain how the reward system aligns with business objectives and how employees can advance their own interests by continuously acquiring knowledge, skills, and abilities and by demonstrating value, as evidenced by exceptional performance, commitment, and teamwork. They also maintain constant communication with employees throughout the performance cycle, to ensure that all employees are aware of how their efforts are impacting the business and what changes are occurring around them that require adjustments in process and/or performance.

Total reward programs provide a mix of base pay, variable pay, and benefits. They are designed with the employee as the primary customer and often with the involvement of employees.

As organizations think more about tying benefits to performance, new offerings are appearing that link performance and employee wants. For example, convenience services are appearing in those organizations where high performance and limited personal time prompt individuals to want laundry services,

---

Don't Assume

Don't assume you know:
- The worth of your employees, as if it could be represented by some fixed percentage of annual income
- What employees need in the way of benefits, recognition, and rewards
- How your employees regard *you*
- Whether your employees understand how you regard *them*
- How employees like their work
- Your employees' personal and professional goals
- How aware employees are of the business goals and objectives for your organization
- How satisfied employees are with their total reward program
- How motivated employees are in general and with working for your organization in particular

Don't assume. Ask!

grocery shopping services, dependent care services, legal and financial planning services, flex time, paid time off benefits, etc. High-performing individuals need and want such offerings, and such services can be offered as rewards and alternative forms of recognition.

Variable pay programs provide employees with the ability to perform at the level of performance they desire. If the design of the program is aligned with the overall financial performance of the organization and pay is linked to results, employees should participate in the distribution of wealth. Savvy managers know the importance of providing a return to employees based on their "investment of self."

Rewarding for the Right Reasons

It's interesting to look at performance review forms for some organizations and the rating factors used by managers. They include such items as:

- Attendance
- Appearance
- Punctuality
- Safety awareness
- Positive attitude
- Work quality
- Work quantity

Pretty basic stuff! And yet not the sort of factors that *drive* results, *improve* performance, *increase* profitability, *enhance* customer retention, and *build* long-term growth. Small wonder wage adjustments in this sort of system are restricted to simple percentage increases in base pay in the form of "merit" raises. Performance reviews in such organizations are dependent upon the *subjective* opinions of immediate supervisors on matters that are of slight significance. But, in fact, these elements should be regarded as givens just to *get into* the game. *Adding value* and *driving change* are the critical success factors required to *stay* in the game of the new workplace over time.

Don't Make This Mistake

Joan was new in her post and wanted to outshine her predecessor by raising "serious" money for her agency. Coordinating every fundraising event and networking with every stakeholder, she exceeded the prior year's results by more than 35%—the second-highest performance in the agency's history. In her annual salary review, she was shocked—and angered—to receive a 3.5% increase. No amount of logic could dissuade the powers that be. Over the next two years, irrespective of results, she received 3.5% increases. Joan's quietly looking … and the agency will soon be, too.

In the new workplace, employees will be prompted to manage the personal corporation of "Me, Myself, and I" with greater savvy and a more vested interest in its financial welfare. As free agent/employees, members of the Net Generation, and other workforce constituents interact in the new workplace, smart managers will be challenged to maintain their interests and retain their talents—and one of the key strategies for doing that will be by rewarding for the right reasons.

Why Rewards Fail

When you come right down to it, belief in the "power of money" is fundamental to our economic system here in the United States. Logically, that would explain why so many hold to the theory that money motivates people to perform in certain ways. But, as we've discussed, not everyone subscribes to that belief. Perhaps these "point" and "counterpoint" exchanges will sound familiar and show the plausibility of both sides of the argument:

Point: "If you throw enough money at a problem, you can fix anything."
Counterpoint: "You can throw as much money as you want; it won't fix *this* problem."

Point: "There isn't anything money can't buy."
Counterpoint: "Money can't buy everything. For example, it can't buy good health, happiness, or even loyalty."

Point: "Every man or woman has his or her price."
Counterpoint: "I can't be bought at any price."

Point: "Everything's for sale."
Counterpoint: "I'm not for sale."

Make the carrot—or, implicitly, the stick—big enough and you can influence or scare almost anyone into doing something. But that approach works to the detriment of all concerned. It creates negative perceptions: "chiefs" are seen as manipulative and distrustful, employees are seen as self-centered, and customers as used. That approach causes long-term benefits to be sacrificed for short-term gains. But nowhere in the equation does the use of the carrot or the stick result in *motivation*.

The problem with most reward systems is the emphasis on rewards. For example, commissioned sales representatives have been known to advance paperwork on sales to make their numbers or hold back sales to a subsequent selling period to meet quota. Multinational corporations and international organizations have made headline news over bribing some official in order to "get the contract" or "land the deal"—all in the name of "winning," making the numbers, getting the recognition. In the

---

CAUTION!

Going, Going, Gone!

Rewards for employees can cause risks for the company. Here's an example of this dynamic. Mike and Carol were shopping for a new car. The salesman offered "assistance." After looking at several cars, they found one they liked. When the three sat down to "look at numbers," they were joined by another salesman. Then the "hard bargaining" began. Several times they attempted to leave, but the two sales reps pursued the sale—and their commission. At the end of two hours, Mike and Carol bought the car and the two salesmen earned their commission. But the experience was very difficult for Mike and Carol: they were happy with the car but not the "team." They never went back to the dealership and they told others how "pushy" and "hungry" the sales staff was. Eventually, word got around: it was the dealership to avoid. The bottom line is that the company paid a commission for the sale—and has paid a lot more since, in terms of sales lost.

end, focusing only on numbers destroys trust and works against long-term interests.

Many organizations wishing to qualify for the Malcolm Baldrige Award—the national award for excellence—believe they will attract more business with this distinguished seal of approval. Yet countless experts advise companies, appropriately, not to even think about applying unless they are already doing quality work. In other words, the award should be of secondary consideration. It is a form of recognition, rather than just an award, for managerial excellence. Of course, doing quality work will get more business, even without the award. But for companies whose underlying motive is just to attract more business, getting the seal of approval somehow feels like a shortcut around all the "hard" stuff of improving processes, productivity, quality, and customer satisfaction.

It's the same way with workplace rewards. The emphasis should be on establishing lasting relations, building repeat business, producing quality products, and providing excellent service. If rewards distract from the pursuit of these objectives, in the end they fail—because they fail to promote the interests of every key constituent. It is this worst-case scenario that has led prominent authorities to conclude that incentives destroy employee motivation—especially if they prompt employees to do something that is detrimental to their integrity and to the process of responding to a higher purpose, in a sense, "building a better world."

Making Rewards a Non-Issue

Smart managers appreciate the importance of making pay a non-issue. They concentrate on treating employees fairly, paying them well, giving them lots of opportunity to excel, and providing the coaching, support, and encouragement to achieve.

Everything that smart managers do with respect to pay is directed at making pay and rewards the natural consequence of performance and not the drivers of it. Smart managers recognize that people want to do a good job and want to realize greater satisfaction from the creative process of working. Improved abili-

Make Pay a Non-Issue

TRICKS OF THE TRADE

To make base pay and other rewards a non-issue:
- Ensure it is competitive with the external market and equitable internally among positions.
- Don't tinker with pay if performance is satisfactory.
- Focus on performance objectives and organizational goals.
- Communicate about how financial and operational dimensions of the business work.
- Concentrate on ways for individuals and groups to become more proficient.
- Make connections between personal and organizational performance.
- Advocate for the equitable distribution of gains.
- Provide performance feedback separate and apart from salary reviews.

ty, knowledge, and proficiency require employees and managers to "partner" in personal development. Individual employees need to assume full responsibility for their own development, but managers need to be available as teachers and coaches to assist in the process. Moreover, savvy managers have a vested interest in the performance of their employees: good, bad, or indifferent, it is a direct reflection on their abilities as managers.

Above all else, both employees and managers need to *recognize that intrinsic rewards are better than extrinsic incentives.* As human beings, we tend to give more of ourselves to the things and people we love. In the new workplace, more emphasis needs to be placed on matching employees with work they love or will come to love. If people are interested in their work, they will be intrinsically motivated to perform. In other words, though it may be trite to say, the work will be its own reward. And their performance will be infinitely better than if they were assigned to less desirable assignments and/or bribed with extrinsic rewards.

Consequently, enterprising employees and their smart managers find the right match between employees and work responsibilities. Proficient employees should be allowed and encouraged to teach other employees. In so doing, they reap the benefits of being recognized for their abilities and they become even more knowledgeable and proficient in their area of interest.

CAUTION!

"Irrational" Drive

"Economic motive is very important...I like to see killer instinct, properly socialized, of course...and a drive to win that really can be almost irrational at times." That's what one venture capitalist told start-up enthusiasts. Obviously, no investor wants to invest in a losing proposition, but no amount of rhetoric can soften the message here. What do you do if you're a manager in an organization this company wants to invest in? While it's good to want to win and to be very enthusiastic, such rhetoric as this drives a "win at any cost" mentality that is more often than not self-destructive.

The Reward of "Choice"

Any person entering into an employment relationship in the new workplace has to start with the realization, "I'm not a captive agent." It's a subtle thought, but one that is very liberating. If conditions are unacceptable, if managers are abusive, if professional and economic returns are not commensurate with the effort invested, employees can leave. They do not have to stay in an employment situation that has all the markings of a win-lose, codependent, parent-child relationship.

Overhearing two employees complaining about work, a third employee joined in, saying, "You know, no one makes you stay here. You can always leave."

It seemed like a harsh statement at the time—and if the remark had come from a manager, the employees might have construed it as a threat. But, the reality, of course, was that they *could* leave.

Embracing that thought brought a new perspective and made them aware that they had been casting themselves in the role of victims. Changing their paradigm helped them realize that the problems they were concerned about were, in a different light, challenges to be tackled head on—or left behind, as the case may be. Savvy managers, too, have changed their paradigm and their approach to working with employees: they regard them not as captives but as free agents in partnership with their managers.

Designing recognition and reward programs capitalizes on the model of employees as free agents, by incorporating options that speak to their abilities and their desire to make decisions that are in their own best interests. Having choices makes employees more willing—call it motivation—to participate in advancing the interests of the organization. Having choices also allows them to see the direct relationship of their endeavors to organizational performance and to the value of their personal stake in the organization's economic fortunes.

Savvy managers invite employees to participate. They appeal to their interests and challenge their abilities with meaningful assignments and suggest ways in which they can become more knowledgeable, more proficient, and ready for even bigger challenges. They allow employees to take courses, to participate in workshops and training programs, and to pursue knowledge in other ways. Indeed, the approach of savvy managers gives employees more power over their future with the understanding that choice, in itself, is an intrinsic reward.

People feel motivated when rewards are a natural consequence of *free choice*. Rewards fail when they are instruments of manipulation and punishment. Enlightened managers understand these things. And they actively seek out employees who have the emotional and professional smarts to thrive in an environment of choice.

Manager's Checklist for Chapter 8

❑ Rewards carry both explicit and implicit messages. What you present in the way of rewards can reflect both positively and negatively on you as a manager.

❑ Pay people fairly and provide them ample opportunity to share in the wealth of the organization.

❑ Compensation invariably relates to performance. Regard pay as a natural consequence of performance and not a driver of it.

❏ Ensure that your reward programs offer many options from which employees can choose. Their choice to work for you and your organization should prove rewarding in and of itself.

❏ Be sure you understand the needs and wants of your employees. Involve them in the initial design and ongoing operations of your total reward program.

❏ Focus on performance and not on rewards. Communication and extensive sharing of information are vital to the overall understanding and enhancement of both personal and organizational performance.

❏ If you offer incentives, provide a blend of both short- and long-term rewards to ensure ongoing recognition of employee performance.

Intrinsic
Rewards

It is imperative for managers to understand the value of intrinsic rewards in the new workplace, because intrinsic rewards are key to unlocking the power of personal motivation. As we indicated earlier, motivation is an *inside* job. As a manager, you cannot "motivate" anyone to do anything. You can force them, you can coerce them, you can bribe them, you can attempt to energize them, but in the end you cannot motivate them.

Motivation has to come from within. Certainly, you influence and can encourage others—we've given lots of suggestions along those lines. And we've cautioned repeatedly against trying to manipulate others by using extrinsic rewards or by treating rewards as anything other than a natural outcome of doing good work. But to understand the essence of intrinsic rewards is to understand the mystery of self-actualization.

In this chapter we'll examine various aspects of intrinsic rewards, and we'll consider examples of what others have done along these lines. But here, too, there's a caution. If you approach the subject of intrinsic rewards as "just another program" or some list of items to be used for getting others to do what you want, you'll have missed the whole point.

Intrinsic rewards must be approached from an employee's perspective and from a values perspective. They are discovered by managers who are willing to join in partnership with their employees. We touched upon several areas of values and intrinsic rewards in Chapter 1, when we discussed the interests of employees as exemplified by the "free agent" of the new workplace.

For intrinsic rewards to be valuable, they must be of value to *employees*. And, even though there will be some "price" placed upon them ultimately by our capitalistic system, enlightened managers understand the critical importance of *unlinking* intrinsic rewards from the extrinsic forms of incentives.

For example, knowledge is very important—not just in business but in life. An *intrinsic* reward with respect to knowledge is the satisfaction of mastering some area of *learning*. An *extrinsic* reward, in this regard, places an economic value on learning, such as with pay-for-knowledge or skill-based pay programs. If managers automatically move to the *extrinsic* payouts for learning and neglect the *intrinsic* value of the process, they lose one of the key elements to unlocking motivation. You don't want employees learning just for *your* sake. You want them learning for *their* sake. That's much more powerful. Moreover, for knowledge to be motivating to employees, it must be of value to them: it must be something they want to learn. Once employees understand the intrinsic value of new skills and knowledge, they are motivated to learn more. The following serves to illustrate this point.

An accounting administrator is invited to go as a company representative to a seminar on a new software system. The purpose of the trip is to learn everything about the system that the company will be using and to be able to train others. The individual is motivated to go—the subject matter is outside her normal sphere of work, so it's a nice change of pace; she wants to learn more about technical systems; and she's flattered to be the one trained as the subject expert for orienting others in the organization. In addition to the *intrinsic* value she places on this training, there would be an *extrinsic* value expressed in the form of financial recognition if she were to receive extra compensation

Intrinsic reward Anything that is satisfying and energizing in itself. Examples include:
- A challenging project that excites the employee and offers lots of opportunity for learning and personal growth
- Participating in a week-long seminar involving timely information on a particular subject of great personal interest
- Assignment to a special project with a team of unique and interesting people
- The opportunity to represent the organization at an outside event

Of course, these experiences should not be imposed on employees. An intrinsic reward should involve choice, personal interest, and enjoyment.

for her newly acquired knowledge or a bonus for taking on the assignment. If the emphasis were primarily on extrinsic rewards (compensation or formal recognition only), employees like this administrative staff member might be influenced to learn only what they're paid to learn—and they would lose the intrinsic value of learning as its own reward.

There are those who pour themselves into their work because they find it energizing, engaging, challenging, even inspiring. Others approach the workweek with dread and count the hours 'til quitting time or eagerly await getting over the mid-week "hump" and then reaching TGIF (Thank God it's Friday!) so they can leave the job behind for another weekend. What accounts for the difference between these two perspectives? The answer lies in the intrinsic appeal—or lack thereof—of the work and the motivation that results.

Enthusiasm is a valuable commodity. Do everything you can as a manager to protect it, nurture it, spread it, capitalize on it. It's the best catalyst for finding how to make work more meaningful.

But don't overlook elements of *structure* and *con-*

Killing Enthusiasm

Many people just starting a job are enthusiastic about the opportunities and the challenges, about a new place and new people and new experiences. Unfortunately, that feeling and their motivation can fade, sometimes very quickly. Savvy managers understand the value of keeping the spirit alive.

tent—structure as represented by the system and *content* by the actual substance of the job itself. Managing these elements properly, as we've discussed before, can improve the intrinsic value of work exponentially.

Meaningful Work

Ask anyone in the workforce today if his or her job is meaningful and you're bound to get an array of responses, from "Mostly" to "You gotta be kidding!" Rarely is the response "Absolutely!"

How motivated do you think people are about their work when their response is anything but "Absolutely!"? I'm not suggesting that it's possible to be 100% motivated 100% of the time. We all feel low on motivation from time to time. But more often the lack of enthusiasm is a commentary on the work people are doing. If the work has little or no intrinsic appeal, how can anyone feel *passion* about doing it? Moreover, because the concept of employment and financial security with any one organization is a thing of the past, employees are seeking the "psychic" and "intellectual" opportunity for meaningful work. Such work appeals to their sense of personal mission and values, while adding to their knowledge base and economic worth in the labor market.

Martha Finney, a veteran business journalist, has been writing about work in America for over 15 years. Co-author of *Find Your Calling, Love Your Life*, she spent more than 12 months on a cross-country driving tour to interview Americans who love their work. Finney recounted to us how struck she was by the sense of mission and dignity exhibited by emergency workers in the aftermath of the bombing of the Oklahoma City Federal building. "Their work was heartbreaking," she reported, "but in the midst of all the wreckage and pain there was hope, caring, and compassion." Finney's message is one that encourages all of us to find a "calling" in what we do.

Creating meaningful work is a responsibility that employee and manager share. Aligning vocation with avocation is certainly idealistic, but it is highly desirable—and more achievable than most would suspect.

Evidence from any number of organizational studies suggests that as much as 40% of an employee's job typically may be "non-value-adding," i.e., work that is not aligned with the strategic objectives of a functional area or organization. (Chapter 4 discusses "value" and "non-value-adding work.") Study data also reveal that employee jobs are highly fragmented in most instances, with an excessive number of tasks and limited responsibility and authority. Inefficient organization structures, restricted technology applications, outdated work processes, and poor people practices are systematically robbing most organizations of their full potential.

Savvy managers understand that to capitalize on the intrinsic value of *meaningful* work they must:

- Encourage employees to identify the energizing aspects of their work and to discover their personal "calling."
- Move employees to where they will learn the most for themselves and for their organizations.
- Position employees where they will contribute the greatest good.
- Link employee interests and personal mission with those of the organization.
- Increase the "value-added" content of employees' work responsibilities by fostering continuous improvement.
- Strive for 80% to 90% alignment between their employees' work and organizational objectives.
- Advocate "whole job" or "whole process" responsibilities to foster an overall sense of employee ownership for the work they perform.

Kathy's Mission

For Example It was something about the way she looked when talking about her job—a sense of peace, an inner calm. Kathy had left her nursing position in the oncology department of a large regional hospital to work for less pay with patients in a hospice setting. Asked by a friend, "How do you do it? Don't you get burned out?," she replied, "I wouldn't dream of doing anything else." Kathy's job was meaningful to her—both in its mission of "healing" and in its impact on the quality of life for those with terminal illness.

- Help their employees make the connection between their work and the larger environment in which the organization operates.

Our capitalistic system has been primarily *exclusive* rather than *inclusive*. In *Leadership Is an Art*, Max De Pree writes, "It [the capitalist system] has been built primarily around contractual relationships, and it has excluded too many people from both its process and a generally equitable distribution of results. The issue here is much more than financial reward: most people never get the opportunity to be *meaningfully involved* (emphasis added) in the working of the system" (pp. 64-65).

Intelligent managers know that for employees to realize the *intrinsic* rewards of *meaningful* work they must be:

- Allowed the opportunity to "spawn upstream," so to speak, to find fertile ground in the form of interesting work assignments.
- Involved in redesigning processes and job responsibilities.
- Included in decisions that impact them directly.

To do otherwise is to invite the hidden costs of increased turnover, absenteeism, lower productivity, and undiscovered ideas.

Learning

Mentioning the words "training and development" in tight economic times is like waving a red flag in many organizations. "Training is the first budget to be cut in our company," remarks a corporate training director. One reason training is often vulnerable to the budgetary ax is that is commonly perceived as an extra, an element that is not critical for increasing productivity and profitability. And, frankly, in some organizations training hasn't demonstrated its relevance to bottom-line business performance. The other reason is that "training" has been *dissociated* from "learning." Of course, the outcome of training *is* learning, and learning directly benefits people and organizations by strengthening needed skills and competencies.

Oddly enough, in the new workplace, learning is one of the principal "rewards" employees seek. They know their immediate and long-term value is linked to their ability to learn new skills and new ideas that will help to keep their "employability" factor high. Learning is the new currency for many free agent/ employees—and it's one of the most meaningful rewards managers can provide.

In reality, learning is an area that has paid high returns for many organizations. Those maximizing returns on their training investment have tended to view learning as an activity that adds value and is therefore an important focus of strategic action. From Motorola University (Motorola), Hamburger University (McDonald's), and Disney University (Disney) to the University for People (Southwest Airlines), Apple University (Apple Computer), and the Aetna Institute for Corporate Education (Aetna), learning has played a major role in the growth and development of some pretty successful organizations! But even the heavy hitters are "rethinking" the process, as learning moves from traditional classroom settings to more on-site, online, real-time environments.

Much of the training and development activity in the U.S. has occurred at the managerial level, which makes up less than 10% of the workforce. Although the estimated amount spent on training is between $45 and $50 billion annually, it is reaching fewer than half of our workers. The advent of pay-for-knowledge and skill-based pay programs has helped to increase the emphasis on employee skills and abilities, but the effects of these initiatives are limited by their focus on specific tasks. And these initiatives and incentive programs neglect many areas of learning, as if to say they're not important or of limited value. The fact is that learning is of enormous value. And both free agents and savvy managers understand the economic "currency" and intrinsic value of learning better than most of their peers.

Yet, the risks associated with lost opportunities for learning represent a serious problem in the face of corporate downsizings and the increased use of contract labor. If there aren't enough

---

Emphasize Learning

Smart managers value learning—for both their employees and their organizations. They promote the intrinsic value of learning by:
- Emphasizing the importance of learning, particularly systems learning and team learning
- Encouraging employees to take advantage of learning opportunities
- Developing in-house and in-service programs to promote communication and cross-functional learning
- De-emphasizing the importance of receiving pay for learning
- Continually identifying subjects worth knowing
- Making resources—books, tapes, speakers, courses—available to employees
- Promoting both individual and collaborative learning
- Helping employees make connections between what they're learning and the benefits for them and the organization

---

people with the skills, knowledge, and ability to drive performance, organizations can't successfully compete. Smart managers understand the importance of retaining valued knowledge and do everything possible to protect this asset. Indeed, there is a dual benefit to doing so. First, their organizations benefit by preserving intellectual capital. Second, employees find intrinsic value in learning—it is motivating for them in that it provides variety and enhances their personal and professional stature.

Creating a learning environment also helps build trust throughout the organization, particularly when it involves all employees. Employees tend to feel more confident in working with each other as trust in the skills of coworkers increases. In his book, *The Human Equation* (1998), Jeffrey Pfeffer references growing evidence that the loss of skills and the increased use of contract employees have hurt productivity and even safety in organizations and industries (pp. 172-173).

Smart managers appreciate the importance of including employees in the process of designing learning experiences. If the subject matter interests employees, if it's relevant to what they do, if the learning helps to build their knowledge and make them more effective, and if it indirectly increases their market value, it will be intrinsically rewarding.

Making History

Ever want to be a "legend" in your own time? Here's how. Value your employees, appreciate the talents that make them special, and recognize accomplishments that stand out "above and beyond the call of duty."

In many organizations there are stories about employees performing larger-than-life feats on the job, stories that have entered into organizational folklore to be passed on from generation to generation. Such legends serve two purposes: they frame an inherent value or a standard and they recognize an employee or employees as exemplifying that value or standard.

In *Leadership Is an Art,* Max De Pree talks about "giants"— "people like you and me" who "see opportunity where others see trouble" and have "special gifts" (p. 73 ff.). Here's what he says to celebrate somebody at Herman Miller as a legend, a giant:

> Giants catch fastballs. One of the giants at Herman Miller is . . . Pep Nagelkirk, who is probably the most talented model maker I have ever heard of . . . He has a special gift for translating ideas and sketches into prototypes. He is an indispensable part of every design program we launch. He is a fastball catcher. Now a fastball may be enough for a pitcher, but it is never enough for a team. Corpora-tions and people can throw good ideas around as often as they want. Without giant catchers like Pep Nagelkirk, those ideas may eventually disappear.

When the president of the company recognizes an employee, that show of appreciation inspires everyone in the organiza-

On-Time Delivery

Federal Express tells the story of the driver who encountered a drop box that he couldn't open. Unable to retrieve the contents from the box, he managed to hoist the entire unit onto his trunk and then drove his truck—drop box and all—back to the terminal to make his scheduled return. Of course, no one knew how he managed to uproot the drop box, but the point in telling the story is to underscore the standard of "on-time" delivery by Federal Express and the passion its employees feel for honoring that standard.

tion. Employees feel motivated to make more of their talents when they know that others appreciate them.

Here's another example. When John G. McCoy was chairman of Bank One, he used to brag about his chief marketing officer, John Fisher. "John's got a great average. Not every hit is a home run; but when he scores one, it's out of the ballpark." Fisher was one of McCoy's giants. And his ability to translate ideas into business helped establish Bank One early on as one of the leading processors of credit card transactions in the industry. Fisher was valued by his chairman and publicly recognized for his creativity.

Smart managers value people and appreciate the gifts that make them and their organizations so special. They understand the intrinsic value of recognizing people for the accomplishments that help to make them "legendary."

One of the qualities of instructional leaders is that of story telling. Instructional managers appreciate that story telling enables them to recognize contributions and communicate desired standards without appearing directive or critical of employees who may not be exhibiting "giant" behavior. Story telling puts the focus on the message and not on the listeners. Furthermore, it allows others to imagine how they can contribute to the traditions of the organization without feeling compelled to follow in the footsteps of a giant. It gives them permission to innovate and contribute in ways that are uniquely theirs. Story telling is an inclusive process that invites others to join in and help make

---

Hunt for Giants

Smart managers begin with the end in mind by first identifying desired outcomes, e.g., *on-time* delivery, *accurate* reporting, product *innovation,* customer *satisfaction.* Then they look for employees who are delivering those specific outcomes— and other outcomes, as well, that are equally desirable. Smart managers collect stories about their "giants" and initiate oral traditions to recognize both the individuals and their heroic feats. Smart managers build "halls of fame" to maximize the intrinsic value of recognizing employees and building honored traditions for future entrants to the new workplace.

> ## No Customer Parking Here
> Avoid trivializing "giant" behavior with gimmicks. Real recognition involves personal appreciation, group recognition, and entry into the annals of the greats. Be attentive to how your employees feel about forms of recognition. For example, maybe they all aspire to being recognized as "Employee of the Month" on a plaque on the wall or gaining a privileged parking space for the month—or maybe they find the plaque or the space pretentious or otherwise bogus. Don't assume: it's your responsibility to know how they feel. Finally remember you don't really want an employee of the month. What you want is for all your employees to be doing great work, so be careful using such programs. They can create resentment among those who weren't so recognized. Instead, recognize individuals and groups whenever they perform well.

the organization something greater than the sum of its members. It sets direction rather than dictating, influences rather than manipulating, motivates rather than demoralizing.

Making history requires planning, discipline, vision, and ongoing recognition—especially recognition of those who are continuing to make history. Just as tribal story telling and the immortalizing of giants play a critical role in defining the culture of Herman Miller, so too the four mandates of founder Walt Disney have built an enduring culture for the Disney Company: *Dream. Believe. Dare. Do.*

Those four magical words for the Disney organization have provided a template for the collective energy and creativity of employees since the founding of the company in 1923. Walt and Roy Disney were certainly giants among giants, but these exhortations of performance have served to inspire teams of artists and production professionals to create legendary characters like Mickey Mouse and Donald Duck and such film classics as *Pinocchio* and *Snow White*. Today, Disney is a multinational corporation of film studios, theme parks, cruise line, resorts, vacation homes, restaurants, retail stores, a learning institute, and much, much more.

The Disney culture is truly a "defining culture," as we discussed in Chapter 5. What is so phenomenal about this culture is the intrinsic reward employees experience in entertaining customers and serving guests. The four-step mandate inspires and energizes employees by linking personal, professional, and organizational goals in a way that is intrinsically powerful. Indeed, being part of a magical world has a magic all its own— because the culture not only recognizes individuals but also reinforces a "total team" concept.

Building Value

As we've discussed, job security is a thing of the past. Today's employment contract can best be described as a "one-day" contract, as Jack Welch, General Electric's CEO, called it, as cited in *The Career Is Dead: Long Live the Career* (1996). The terms of that contract are defined by how much value the employer and employee each bring to the relationship. If an employer isn't building the free agent/employee's portfolio of skills and, therefore, market worth; if extrinsic rewards aren't commensurate with the value added; if employees aren't making a difference every day, then all bets are off. Employees can walk or they can be terminated— merged, downsized, outsourced, or other-sourced, as with a professional employer organization that might assume the former employees under a new umbrella. Either way, *adding value* is key to the relationship—for both parties.

So how do organizations build value over time and keep employees growing? One answer suggests there is significant potential in the intrinsic reward of "space"—the opportunity to excel.

Savvy managers build value for employees and their organizations by:

- Offering work that has meaning and purpose
- Providing experiences for increased learning
- Offering "space," i.e., opportunities to achieve
- Encouraging beneficial relationships
- Making sure employees have all the resources needed to do their work successfully
- Respecting and trusting their ability and willingness to achieve

The Gift of Space

Max DePree recounts in *Leadership Is an Art* the early days of Herman Miller when his dad felt at fault for not being able to pay commissions owed to his sales representatives. He was visiting the home of one of his key reps and recalled, "Jim's family would have no Christmas." But Jim had an upbeat recollection: "For Marion and me it was one of the highlights of our lives." It was on that visit that DePree gave Jim the New York sales territory, which Jim called "the greatest opportunity I've ever had." Jim had received the gift of space.

- Intrinsically and extrinsically rewarding desired performance

Savvy managers understand the value of growing people and facilitate the process by networking them throughout the systems in which they work. Networking benefits both employees and their managers. It adds to the shared base of learning and influence for both and establishes a connectivity that is potentially beneficial to all parties, in both the short and longer term.

Networking and connectivity develop *relational* influence, which is now more important than *organizational* influence, according to Douglas T. Hall (*The Career Is Dead*). Relational activity tends to provide more intrinsic value for employees than organizational activity in that it provides personal support as well as learning and work opportunities, but on a smaller scale. Consequently, the intrinsic value of networks and relational activity cannot be overlooked—or underestimated.

Smart managers know that building value requires recognition of not only the giants in their midst—and *everyone* is a giant at one time or another—but also the teams of employees who make it happen every day. Team recognition helps to build value by drawing employees of differing backgrounds and interests into a cohesive whole. As we discussed in Chapter 7, teams—like those at Apple, who invented the Macintosh, and Southwest Airlines, who continue to bring acclaim to the carrier—are vitally important to the success of an organization.

Consequently, when smart managers focus on relational activity, they actually are providing intrinsic rewards to employees

Key Term **Relational influence** A phenomenon of interdependency, of being in mutually beneficial relationships. The old saw, "To get ahead, it's not *what* but *whom* you know," is being replaced by a newer version: "In today's workplace it takes *whom* you know *and what* you know to get *anywhere*." Relational development consists of advancing through increasingly complex levels of interdependency, rather than through individual achievements, to reach some level of independence and differentiation. Smart employees know that their ability to survive and their resilience depend on developing sound relationships and collaborative models of mutual learning and influence.

and extrinsic value to their organizations. As employees influence, train, and support one another, they grow individually and as a group and, in turn, bring value to their work projects, business units, and organization.

For Example **Mapping the Future** Returning from an off-site planning retreat, Tricia and Kelly Burke decided to make a difference by embarking on a journey to transform their entire business. Part of their vision included changing their main office supply and furniture operation to a "customer solutions center." To introduce the plan, Tricia worked with the local AAA office to create a Triptik® showing the target dates and envisioned steps, including "bumps" in the road—"renovation" of the selling floor—and cross-functional "team" training events. By investing in a little creativity and time, they demonstrated respect and caring for their employees.

Personal Integrity

Just as continuous employment and financial security with any one employer are a thing of the past, so too are personal careers, as we've known them. With the uncertainty of employment relationships and waning promises of career fulfillment, many employees are internalizing their concept of career. They're attempting to integrate personal values and their work with a purposeful life.

This trend of personalizing careers is resulting in highly variable and extremely multifaceted pictures. Rather than some general area of specialization or specific professional path, careers are tending to look more like life plans, embracing all aspects of an individual's personal and professional interests

Integrity The state of being whole or entire. Although we tend to use the word "integrity" as synonymous with honesty, which certainly is a very valuable commodity, the base meaning of the word suggests "having it all together" (rough translation). In other words, all aspects of one's being—personal, professional, spiritual, public, private, and so on—form a whole. Consequently, with all aspects totally integrated, a person can be true to himself or herself and honest with others. In the new workplace, appealing to an employee's integrity is intrinsically rewarding. It invites the employee to commit to performance and offers alignment with the person's interests and sense of self-worth, mission, values, and ideals.

and ideals, as more and more free agent/employees search for meaning as well as compensation for their services.

Consequently, smart managers must appeal to the values, ideals, and interests of their employees within the context of their employees' life plans. But, above all else, every employee's stock in trade is and will be his or her personal integrity.

Personal integrity requires workers to be able to access themselves, to stay grounded when everything around them is shifting and coming apart. It requires them to think in terms of varied experiences, continuous learning, and constant uncertainty. They must also regard work as boundaryless, just like the organization described by General Electric CEO Welch, where boundaries of authority, tasks, politics, and identity are constantly changing. At a minimum, it requires a commitment to "living by one's wits."

Smart managers appreciate the difference they make in the workplace. Yet sometimes they don't realize how much influence they actually have. Suffice it to say, anytime employees express unhappiness over pay, benefits, and/or working conditions, it's usually a substitute issue for "management." Usually, it's because some inflexible, inconsiderate, hard-nosed, purple-eyed, people-eating "boss" hasn't done what enlightened managers do, i.e., communicate with employees and collaborate on addressing needs. In fact, from our experience in labor and employee relations matters, it's usually the *intrinsic* and not so

Integrity, Not Loyalty

Savvy managers understand that loyalty is dead. For it to exist, there must be a commitment and a willingness to overcome any difficulties that threaten to separate parties who choose to remain in a relationship. In the past, employers demanded loyalty of their employees. Rarely was there reciprocity, with a few notable exceptions. But all that's changed. Today there is no loyalty—on either side of the table. But employees and employers should expect *integrity* from one another. Savvy managers emphasize building trust and enhancing personal and interpersonal integrity. It's intrinsically rewarding—and imperative!

much the *extrinsic* stuff that angers employees. Conversely, the *intrinsic* aspect of recognizing and rewarding employees is usually more effective than the *extrinsic*.

Organizational Pride

In the new workplace, where relational influence is more meaningful than organizational influence, smart managers are working diligently to recruit people who take pride in their work and to create teams of people who aspire to accomplishments in which they can take pride.

- *It's indescribable!* Nations have it! Professional sports teams have it! Organizations that stand out in their marketplace have it!
- *It's intangible!* Wall Street doesn't value it! Investors usually don't care about it! Most CEOs don't shout about it!
- *It's desirable!* Managers know about it! Employees seek it and know when they've got it! Customers benefit from it!

The "it" is organizational pride—and it's made some pretty small and large companies very, very successful!

One of the most significant areas for intrinsic reward is an organization's system of values and guiding principles. Companies like Ben & Jerry's and Patagonia espouse values that relate to stewardship of our societal and natural environment. The Ben & Jerry's Foundation makes quarterly donations at its board's discretion of approximately 7.5% of its pre-tax profits and offers competitive grants to not-for-profit, grassroots organizations throughout the United States. The company also sponsors Community Action Teams led by its employees. Patagonia donates 1% of all sales to environmental activism. Employees seeking to align their personal values with organizational values actively pursue employment opportunities with companies like these.

Similarly, employees seeking family-friendly organizations are checking out companies that have flexible schedules, daycare and eldercare resources, jobsharing, and other family-friendly policies. Gay men and lesbians are seeking companies that are accepting of them. And many employees are interested in the "top 100 best companies to work for in America" (after the book by the same title) and any organizations that are close to fitting that description. In a word, "pro-people" companies tend to offer both the *intrinsic* and the *extrinsic* rewards many employees seek. Moreover, employees of such organizations are proud to be affiliated with enterprises espousing values that they share.

One final thought: in a complex and changing workplace, many employees are caught in a struggle to produce quality products and services, while watching their jobs go away. They're proud of the work they and their teams produce, but they're growing more resentful about doing more with less. Team spirit may be up, but organization pride is questionable. Enlightened managers are encouraging employees to focus on the positive, manage the anger, and be proud of what they are accomplishing—individually and as teams. Particularly in this context, enlightened managers are providing intrinsic value by what *they* bring to the table, by supporting their employees and walking beside them.

Manager's Checklist for Chapter 9

❑ Intrinsic rewards represent a cache of influence for savvy managers. From interesting work assignments to constructive personal behavior, the possibilities are limitless.

❑ Divining and designing meaningful work is your most effective way of helping your employees fulfill their personal and professional goals. It's the most intrinsic reward of all.

❏ Learning is a lifelong process of continued growth and development. Look for ways to foster mutual learning in particular. It's a win-win for everyone.

❏ The most effective way to build value in any organization is to provide enterprising employees with "space," i.e., opportunity.

❏ Learn the value of relational influence. Networking and connecting are important processes to ensure ongoing support, communication, and growth.

❏ Employees in the new workplace are seeking meaning in their work and in their lives. Linking personal and organizational values provides intrinsic rewards for many employees.

Extrinsic Rewards

In contrast with intrinsic rewards, extrinsic rewards are those "satisfiers" that come from the external environment in which we work or live. Extrinsic rewards in the workplace include various forms of compensation, such as base pay and incentives, benefits, and other cash and cash equivalents. The combination of base pay, incentives, and benefits is often referred to as the "total reward program."

At one level, extrinsic rewards are recompense for work performed and serve to satisfy our basic requirements for survival. At another level, they provide the means to live "comfortably" by meeting "wants" that are above the level of "need." But at the other end of the spectrum is a level of reward that is unlimited, in a sense. For most people, the concept of unlimited extrinsic rewards is unrealistic, unimaginable, unthinkable! The allure is seductive, but the likelihood for most is so remote as to be dismissed immediately as impossible.

Money and other extrinsic rewards are regarded as "motivators" by many managers and compensation wizards, but opposing views in other circles of management study have long held that

Extrinsic rewards
Systems of recognition that are provided by persons other than the employee/free agent for services rendered. They may take the form of base pay programs, variable pay plans, bonuses, incentives, prizes, cash, cash equivalents, benefits, gainsharing plans, profit-sharing plans, commissions, stock options, and alternative pay programs.

such extrinsic rewards are either "satisfiers" or "dissatisfiers" but *not* motivators.*

Extrinsic rewards are extremely important in business, but it seems that too much emphasis has been placed on extrinsic rewards as "motivational tools" and that their use has largely been inappropriate and manipulative, i.e., both rewarding and punishing. Herzberg, Kohn, and others have argued convincingly that motivation derives from the work itself and that employees are motivated to perform better if they're encouraged and supported in developing a constructive and empowering relationship with their work. To help employees develop a deeper sense of pride in themselves and in their work, managers need to give them greater authority in their work. They should also give them direct and individual feedback and expand the scope of their jobs.

But how can extrinsic rewards best be used? And to what extent are they effective in getting employees to increase productivity, profitability, quality, and other desirable outcomes? Is there a limit to their use or a point of diminishing returns? We intend to answer these and other related questions as we examine the subject of extrinsic rewards.

Base Pay and Total Reward Programs

To attract applicants, managers must provide competitive rewards in the form of base pay, benefits, and other incentives. Oftentimes base wages are determined by identifying certain "benchmark" positions that can be readily compared with similar positions in the marketplace. Other internal jobs can then be compared with the benchmarked positions within an organization and clustered into pay grades according to the relative

*Frederick Herzberg, "One More Time: How Do You Motivate Employees?" *Harvard Business Review*, January-February 1968.

worth of each job. The market value for a job usually determines the midpoint of a salary range, with the minimum and
maximum levels of pay being some predetermined percentage
spread from the midpoint.

Managers often refer to this base pay as the employee's "entitlement" for services rendered. But "entitlements" have become
somewhat odious to many institutions. The term connotes a sense
of permanence, something "owed," compensation that employees
may or may not have really earned, like some social welfare program. Of course, in the new workplace, the last thing anyone can
count on is permanence, so the base rate is pretty much the
"required" level of pay for reporting to work every day. But, in
reality, no one is getting a free ride in today's new workplace. Work
is hard, resources are limited, and every effort counts.

Currently, the newer approach to "incenting" employees in
the workplace has to do more with *variable* rather than *fixed*
pay, as we'll discuss later in this chapter. Without addressing the
premise underlying such programs, suffice it to say they signal
a trend away from adding to base pay programs *ad infinitum*.
More specifically, alternative pay programs are becoming
increasingly popular because they represent a clear attempt to
link pay to performance to the greatest extent possible and
because they hold the promise of lower labor costs by influencing workers to become more productive. But difficulties arise
when managers think employees are earning too much and
they proceed to adjust (lower) the allowances.

Other examples of base pay programs include:

- *Straight time hourly income* as a function of an employee's regular weekly rate and the number of hours
  worked
- *Commission sales programs*, in which employees receive
  a fixed or graduated percentage of pay based on achieving certain levels of sales productivity
- *Base rate programs* that, together with tip income, satisfy or exceed minimum wage requirements
- *Fixed-income plans*, as with salaried employees who
  receive a weekly, biweekly, or monthly salary commensu-

> **Key Term**
>
> **Merit** A term suggesting that an employee is deserving of reward or recompense for services performed. In the case of merit increases, a person "merits" an adjustment to base pay, usually because of having done a "good" or even "exceptional" job. The concept of merit pay, however, connotes some inherent attribute akin to that of an "allowance," like that given to a child by some beneficent parent. While managers are inclined to regard merit pay and merit adjustments as performance-related, they tend to be adjustments to what is essentially an entitlement to fair and competitive wages.

rate with the salary grades and exemption requirements for salaried employees

- *Piece-rate plans*, by which employees receive income according to their level of productivity
- *Variable pay plans*, by which employees receive some portion of base pay while the remainder is held back pending achievement of certain individual and/or group results.

Problems with all of these approaches arise when the "pool" for increases is restricted and the resulting distribution of additional pay is limited, regardless of "merit," or when the upper limits appear too "generous" according to someone's subjective opinion and "caps" are imposed or pay formulas are adjusted to reduce the overall income for employees. The effect is to restrict the overall earnings potential of the employee—a condition that often leads to frustration, poor morale, and eventually turnover.

Smart managers concentrate on paying employees appropriately—in terms

> **Caution!**
>
> **Labor Rates vs. Labor Costs**
>
> Managers often confuse labor *rates* with labor *costs*. If employee A is twice as productive as B and both are compensated equally, the labor cost for products produced by A will be half that of B. Even if A were to receive some increment of pay above that for B, so long as productivity remains constant, products produced by A will still have a lower labor cost than those produced by B. Smart managers concentrate on ways to boost productivity—and they're happy to see productive employees earn more. It's just good business.

of both external competitiveness and internal equity. They know that, if employees are not paid fairly and competitively, pay will become a dissatisfier and distract employees from their primary mission of fulfilling customer expectations and achieving company goals. They understand that enlightened compensation practices help to attract and retain valued employees. They view compensation as an "investment" to protect critical knowledge and preserve continuity of organizational performance. Moreover, smart managers recognize that satisfied workers produce! And increased productivity results in lower labor costs and increased profit margins.

Performance Management and Pay for Performance

Performance management systems typically call for managers to rate employee performance according to some set of predetermined criteria—subjective, objective, or both. Ratings are then reviewed for appropriate pay adjustments. Of course, the principle of the infamous "bell curve" is applied, so that pay increases are distributed according to some preapproved pattern; e.g., the bottom 10% of the employees generally receive no increase and perhaps are subject to probationary action, the top 10% receive "exceptional" increases, and the middle 80% receive increases that are "slightly below" or "slightly above" or just plain "average."

As we discussed in Chapter 5, performance reviews are important tools for feedback. Managers should not manipulate them to justify a decision. For example, a manager thinks employee X should get little or no increase, so she writes an uncomplimentary review of X's performance, or she contends that employee Y should receive an outstanding increase and writes the appraisal to justify the recommendation. Sometimes the person to read the review is not the employee but some administrative authority who may need "convincing" to allow the increase desired by the manager for his or her employee. This sort of administrative "politicking" is unfortunate, because the review process should be for the benefit of the employee, to help him or her improve.

It makes sense that performance feedback and pay adjustments should be *unlinked*, for many reasons—and particularly with respect to timing. If the pay system is designed well, it will be able to stand on its own and employees will be able to anticipate the appropriate level of reward based on what they already know about their performance. Unfortunately, a lot of managers insist upon perpetuating the "halo" and "horns" system—where someone gets the "halo" and an outstanding increase based on glowing verbiage in a performance review document or gets the "door" based on some extreme level of feigned dissatisfaction.

While base pay programs such as variable pay and piece-rate plans are intended to link performance and pay, such plans are problematic because they're easy to manipulate, as previously noted. Such systems as gainsharing and profit sharing are more desirable and more equitable in the long run and they allow employees to see a more direct correlation among individual, group, and organizational performance levels.

Pay-for-performance programs are good as a means of distributing rewards commensurate with the level of individual and team effort. But this is noticeably different from the view that such systems are needed to motivate employees. Apart from any short-term influence, they are not motivating *per se*. And managers tending to view such programs as "motivationally" rewarding—and, thereby, punishing, if individuals or teams fail to produce desired outcomes—stand to do long-term harm to morale and to the inherent ability of organizational members to do their best over the long haul.

Performance Reviews

If employees are surprised by your feedback in a performance review session, then either you haven't been communicating or they haven't listened. Review time should be an occasion to document prior communication. In other words, what you've been communicating all throughout the performance cycle should now be reflected in the review documents. And nothing in the review should be *news*—good or bad. Moreover, as discussed in Chapter 5, performance review sessions are opportunities for development and should *not* be used for disciplinary purposes or for communicating concerns for the first time.

Smart managers tend to regard compensation simply as a matter of business. Similarly, they view performance reviews as a subset of a larger system of goal setting, collaborative planning, and feedback—not as merely tools for manipulation or political expediency.

To link pay with performance, there needs to be some clear understanding of what is expected of both individuals and their organizations. Performance management systems make that connection. As plans are developed at the outset of a performance period, goals are identified against which performance can be measured. Smart managers work with their people throughout the period to ensure they have the resources and support they need to be successful.

Separate from the performance management system is the reward program, which is built according to its own set of objectives and performance criteria. With the proper correlation of these two systems and continuous communication, employees are able to determine their relative standing with respect to their personal effectiveness and their eligibility for extrinsic rewards. And, we contend, the more objective these two systems are, the less employees need to be "reminded" of pay consequences and the more they can concentrate on their work and the intrinsic value it offers.

Games, Prizes, and Other Forms of Reward

No one ever said work had to be dull or that work and play were mutually exclusive. In fact, fun and enjoyment at work are energizing, foster creativity, and inherently motivate. As we discussed in Chapter 9, extrinsic rewards of respect and appreciation are extremely valuable—and personally meaningful.

However, many have taken "fun" to new levels, such as with the example cited in Chapter 2, where the "manager of whoopee" was challenged to find new games, contests, and rewards for employees on a continuous basis. The results have not always been that effective and the "fun" has been, at times, somewhat questionable.

Hype or Hypocrisy?

Smart Managing Extrinsic rewards in the form of contests, prizes, and "sudden acts of random recognition" provide additional ways for managers to recognize employees. Such rewards can vary from immediate cash payouts for "good behavior" to grand-prize trips for being "tops" in a performance category. Problems arise when the intention behind such programs is to "stimulate" (substitute the word "manipulate") employees under the guise of "fun." Employee trust for managers goes down—along with long-term performance. Smart managers make work fun, but they avoid the "hoopla" that undermines trust and detracts from the real business of work.

Ask instructional designer Judy Vetovitz of Tricon Global Restaurants about extrinsic rewards and having fun, and you'll get an idea of how both can be effectively linked to energize a culture. "It wasn't always that way," explains Vetovitz. When the company (which includes KFC, Pizza Hut, and Taco Bell) was part of PepsiCo, employees stayed within their own zone of responsibility. "If it wasn't in the job description, people weren't much inclined to go out of their way."

After the spin-off from PepsiCo, CEO David Novak introduced new principles for Tricon. He emphasized the importance of being individually and collectively accountable for business growth, helping one another, and working as a team. Through a series of workshops, employees explored ways to assimilate these tenets, including how they might recognize one another for doing "little extras," for "going above and beyond the call of duty."

Employees were encouraged to fill out a "Walk the Talk" card when they observed or experienced someone going the extra mile. Employee recognition cards are collected from drop boxes around the organization and reviewed for follow-up. If any employee is the subject of at least five recognition cards in a month, a cross-functional team of some 20 employees, each of whom plays an instrument, serenades the unsuspecting employee in front of his or her peers. The band's chorus concludes with "We're here to recognize YOU"—and the performers point to the person being honored. The employees who submitted the recognition cards read them and the honoree receives a "bucket of trinkets and trivets"—inexpensive items like movie tickets, notepads, T-shirts, or other mementos.

Even those who don't get serenaded by the band may be recognized in departmental meetings, as their manager reads some of the cards they've received. "It's not always job-related," Vetovitz notes. "Sometimes an employee may have baby-sat an infant for another employee who'd just had a baby, or maybe someone volunteered personal time and did something special in the way of community service."

Even though the rewards are not "big ticket," the recognition seems to be for the right stuff—positive contributions, teamwork, cooperation, thoughtfulness. Plus those who bestow the compliments are primarily peers, not just bosses. How different this is from other programs, where employees are incented to compete with one another for big prizes and cash payouts, rewards that focus on individual performance and "separateness."

But what about "big ticket" programs? What do they look like? We'll address these questions momentarily. But first let's talk about personal growth and advancement in the new workplace.

Growth and Advancement

Careers are changing. In fact, some argue that the concept of "career" as we've known it is over. As employees move in and out of organizational assignments, "flexibility" has become the watchword.

It used to be that base pay programs, with their elaborate system of pay grades and salary ranges, systematically marked where people were in terms of compensation by virtue of their time and grade. The more time with an organization in a given job, the higher a person could expect to be in his or her pay grade. Once the employee had achieved the top of the range, he or she was locked in until such time as the range was adjusted or the employee was promoted into another grade.

One development in pay systems over the last few years has been the emergence of "pay banding," as we've discussed, allowing greater flexibility and movement according to how job assignments change. Similar concepts are emerging that recognize the acquisition of skills and demonstrated abilities on the job.

In a word, the traditional benchmarks of career advancement—higher job grades and increased pay—are disappearing. Moreover, the migration from entitlement systems to pay-for-performance programs points to the need for employees to demonstrate their value and their unique capabilities—continuously, if they expect to garner the income they think they deserve.

Rather than rewarding individual advancement, smart managers are focusing on how employees are working to advance the group as a whole and how they're using the resources of the group to develop themselves. Rather than valuing individual competence exclusively, smart managers are concerned with how employees are advancing the knowledge of the group overall and growing more knowledgeable in the process. And, rather than rewarding individual performance all by itself, smart managers are focusing on how employees are enhancing group performance collectively. In today's workplace, career advancement and personal growth are subordinate to the growth and advancement of the team and, in turn, the organization as a whole.

Indeed, the shift in emphasis from *entitlement* to *performance* and from *individual* to *team* suggests that smart managers must approach the subject of extrinsic rewards from the perspective of "win-win" rather than "win-lose." Under traditional reward systems, managers were challenged to distribute rewards according to the bell curve—the empirical model for "winners" and "losers." In the new workplace, base compensation plans provide wider

Pay Attention to What You Reward

Don't get caught up with how long someone has been on the job or doing a particular task. Watch for ways in which employees are adding value to the team, the organization, the service reputation of the unit. Just because someone appears to be the "keeper of the keys" with respect to special knowledge or the "gatekeeper" barring anyone else from learning their job is no reason to be intimidated or, worse, to placate them with increases. Regard transfer of knowledge as important as knowledge itself—and reward it.

latitude for paying employees competitively, without the limitations of narrowly defined job grade and salary range systems. The upside for income potential lies in distributing rewards according to "value creation" or "gains in operational and financial performance." Such systems foster a "win-win" environment, where individuals working collaboratively and to the best of their ability are making gains on behalf of the organization as a whole. A logical consequence is a reasonable and equitable distribution of the gains—hence, the emergence of "gainsharing" and "win-sharing" programs, as we'll discuss shortly.

Wealth Creation

Many organizations are moving to better align individual and group performance with the performance of their enterprises as a whole. Consequently, extrinsic reward programs are taking the form of large systems plans, such as profit sharing and stock ownership (particularly for publicly held organizations) and "gainsharing."

The efficacy of such plans lies in the distribution of "gains" or "wealth" created out of the collective efforts of organizational members. Moreover, funding for such programs ebbs and flows according to the fortunes of the organizations. Payment is variable, rather than fixed, and the timing of any distributions is according to the performance cycle of the organization rather than that of the individual.

> **Key Term**
>
> **Large systems plans** Reward programs that affect the organization as a whole, rather than an operational unit, department, or finite functional area. When we talk about "large systems designs," we're referring to structures that are company-wide and generally encompassing 1000 employees or more. With respect to reward programs, "large systems plans" refer to cross-organizational designs such as profit-sharing, win-sharing, and gainsharing plans that consistently link employees to common operational and economic goals.

Smart managers welcome the advent of such plans because it allows them to communicate the fundamentals of the operation or business to employees. By educating and communicating with respect to the "critical success factors" or "profit drivers" of an organization, managers help their employees better understand and cooperate more fully in furthering the success of the group or the enterprise as a whole. Moreover, such plans tend to encourage people to work together for the good of all involved, in contrast with individual performance plans that effectively isolate the performance of the individual from the rest of the organization.

Results of such systems can be spectacular, as we discussed in Chapter 5 with the example of Springfield Remanufacturing Corporation. But, if wealth creation itself becomes the primary focus of the organization, rather than some altruistic mission of "building a better world" or "enriching the lives of others," the results may be disappointing all the way around.

In 1999 United Parcel Service went public with its stock. For the first time ever, "outsiders" were able to invest in UPS. Previously, employees had been allowed to purchase company stock through payroll deduction, but with the public offering employees were able to see how market influences might affect the value of their shares. It was pretty exciting. For UPS—as with other organizations that provide opportunity for employee ownership—there is significant value in aligning employee interests with the economic performance of the company. Imagine how employees might view striking the company for any prolonged period, given the potential adverse impact on stock performance and the value of their personal holdings, or how they might pull together to "best the competition," given the potential positives as related to stock values.

Certainly, with respect to extrinsic rewards, the trend is away from entitlements and merit pay systems and toward performance-based plans and total company performance. And, as the free agent/employee in today's workplace becomes even more savvy in matters involving global economics and wealth creation, the extrinsic rewards of choice will be those provided by large systems plans such as profit sharing, gainsharing, and stock ownership.

Consequently, smart managers are emphasizing the importance of teamwork and maintaining a larger view. They know

Making the Connection

Oftentimes too much emphasis is placed on "betting the farm" or "making the numbers." Indeed, more than one CEO has learned the hard way that a "vision" of increased "return on investment" or being "the most profitable" is not a *vision* but an *objective*—and not particularly inspiring for organizational members. Smart managers enable employees to make the connection between mission and profit by emphasizing the importance of their work, their team, their market, their customer. In fact, organizations that emphasize mission over money outperform the competition every time.

Smart Managing

that by doing so they are benefiting individual employees as well as the overall team with a capital "T." Moreover, both managers and employees are beginning to take the *longer* view as to the value of such rewards, since their worth may vary—particularly when it is tied to some external market factor, such as the stock market.

Short-Term Programs

Short-term reward programs usually focus on immediate or near-term results, within a performance period somewhere in the range of a year or less. And, while some authorities regard programs like profit-sharing and gainsharing plans to be short-term, we tend to regard them as somewhat longer-term because such plans are *system-wide* and *ongoing*. Even though payouts under such programs are usually annual, the ultimate objective of these plans is longer-term, e.g., "profitability" or "improved performance" *continuously over time*.

Extrinsic rewards for the short term include:

- Bonus plans with near-term payouts, e.g., annually, semiannually, quarterly, etc.
- Short-term incentive plans, e.g., performance plans, project rewards, etc.
- Measurement-based plans, where performance measures are determined according to specific objectives, e.g., reduced cycle time, improved quality, etc.
- Cash and cash-equivalent prizes

- Sales incentives such as commissions, bonuses, and other financial rewards for achieving compensable levels of sales performance
- Group incentive plans of all sorts, e.g., team incentives and group recognition plans
- Merger and other event-specific incentive plans
- Stock and stock options for meeting short-term performance expectations or for unplanned yet commendable results
- Re-earnable incentives and other variable pay awards
- Service recognition and other service awards
- Hiring incentives, for referring others and for "signing on"
- Retention incentive programs, plans aimed at reducing turnover or retaining critical expertise
- "On the spot" awards for exhibiting desired behavior or unusual results
- Prizes, gifts, and re-earnable perks for all sorts of reasons

Inherent in the design of short-term reward programs is the concept of *quid pro quo*—"If you do that, you get this" or "Because you were so deserving, we thought you should have these." Payments or distributions may be performance-based or event-specific, but they can also be quite discretionary. Moreover, short-term reward programs tend to target individuals or small groups, while longer-term plans tend to focus on the larger system and results that have a more reaching impact on total organizational performance.

It is crucial to the process of recognition and reward that you as a manager link the *extrinsic* payouts for employee contributions back to the *intrinsic* value of what employees do and the benefit they provide others. Emphasize "mission over money"— as we stated above. If the relationship is strictly *transactional,* without some redeeming quality of "performing to a higher standard" or "building a better world," the result will most assuredly be short-lived.

Short-term plans beget short-term results. As many experts have affirmed, the risk associated with short-term plans is the

potential or actual adverse
impact on longer-term performance. To have longer-
term constructive value, we
contend that the design of
any reward program must
incorporate a strong com-
ponent of *intrinsic* worth:
the work that employees
are doing is worthwhile in
and of itself. Putting everything in context, plan formulas should merely assure
all eligible participants that
the distribution of wealth
will be equitable and consistent with the value created. Beyond that, such plans
should not require further
elaboration. Smart managers concentrate on setting objectives,
providing feedback, and enriching the relationship between
employees and their work.

> ### Time and Action
>
> **Smart Managing**
>
> To optimize the effects of short-term rewards, smart managers identify the desired results, behaviors, or outcomes when the plan is introduced. They make sure that measures or benchmarks are clear and provide independent feedback throughout the performance period. Whatever the measurables of the program, smart managers keep the participants aware of results; for example, if profit objectives are the measurables, they regularly provide reports on the unit's or organization's performance. Payments are timely, relevant, and appropriate and the managers thank the participants their efforts to bring about the desired end.

Longer-Term Programs

Longer-term plans tend to take a longer view with respect to
organizational performance and involve the greatest number of
organizational members. The performance period is somewhere in the range of a year or more. Payouts may be annual,
multi-year, and/or overlapping. Moreover, the design usually
involves some benchmarking, setting levels at which different
levels of payout are triggered, e.g., minimum or threshold,
midpoint or market, and maximum. Implicit in the design of
such plans is funding based on some required level of organizational performance.

For example, in the case of a profit-sharing plan, organizational performance must be at or above a certain level, at which

point some percentage of total profit—however defined—is set
aside to allocate among plan participants based on some formula and according to the extent of their participation. For
many employees, participating in a profit-sharing plan or thrift
savings program represents a far better investment vehicle than
anything on the open market, since companies offering such
plans generally match up to 50% and even 100% of employee
savings to some maximum level of participation.

Such longer-term programs include:

- Profit-sharing plans, initially funding vehicles for pension
  purposes, but now focusing more on bottom-line results
  and with more immediate feedback
- Gainsharing programs, targeting specific areas for productivity improvement and cost savings, usually in a
  manufacturing environment
- Win-sharing plans, similar to gainsharing and other performance-based programs, but defining measures of success largely in terms of financial performance
- Success sharing, an integration of operational and financial performance improvement
- Goal-sharing plans, aimed at reducing costs and adding
  value, which in turn drives plan funding
- Performance-sharing plans, with criteria based on measurable improvements and generally closer to the line of
  vision for employees

TRICKS OF THE TRADE   **Open-Book Management**

To be meaningful to employees, longer-term reward programs
require extensive education, training, support, and ongoing communication. The link between employee understanding and performance
is crucial. Smart managers do everything within their control to ensure
that they and their employees are "experts" in all matters affecting the
operational and financial performance of their organizations. Regardless
of title, pay level, status, or tenure, every member is credited with the
intelligence and ability to impact organizational performance. And their
effectiveness in doing so determines whether additional payouts will be
available over and above their base compensation.

- Longer-term bonus programs, usually based on achieving at least threshold levels of financial performance relative to certain marketplace measures, such as return on investment (ROI) or return on equity (ROE)
- Stock plans, including ESOPs (employee stock ownership plans) and restricted stock, which encourage awareness of the economic drivers and market value of the enterprise
- Performance trusts, usually funded according to some "set-aside" for distribution based on achieved levels of performance
- Phantom stock programs, generally based on financial improvement according to some level of assumed financial value in the marketplace

Whether short-term or longer-term, rewards are an increasingly important part of life in the new workplace. Smart managers know that to unite the efforts of "owned" and contract employees, they must provide total reward programs that align individual and group interests with those of the larger system and they must link both the extrinsic and the intrinsic value of work to optimize organizational performance.

Risk Sharing and Reward Sharing

It could be argued that employees should share in the risks as well as the rewards of an organization's economic fortune. As noted above, it can be pretty exciting when everything is on the upswing. But the downside potential can be terrifying—if not downright tragic.

Consider the plight of the more than 42,000 employees of Vencor, one of the nation's largest chains of hospitals and nursing homes. When the company declared bankruptcy in 1999, the fortunes of many employees—as represented by their 401(k) plan and stock purchase program—virtually evaporated.

Encouraged by the performance of the stock in its startup years, employees eagerly invested their personal income in company stock through the convenience of payroll deduction. And, following a one-year waiting period, new employees could

> **⚠ CAUTION!**
>
> **Risk Management**
>
> Any investor understands the danger of putting all of his or her eggs in one basket. Managing risk requires spreading investments across a range of vehicles, e.g., equities, bonds, diverse industries, domestic investments, and foreign investments—all according to the degree of risk tolerance and the goals of the individual investor. Similarly, the design of long-term reward programs that are aligned with company interests must incorporate certain safeguards that mitigate against "betting the farm" on one and only one investment vehicle.

enroll in the company's 401(k) plan, with company stock as one of the investment options. Employee contributions to the plan were, of course, matched by Vencor with company shares. The aggressive employee investors who put all of their money in company stock suffered, as both personal and company contributions collapsed in value.

Smart managers appreciate the value of plan safeguards to help manage risk. And, while it's entirely laudable to distribute wealth, employees do not have ultimate control for determining individual and organizational fate, so they should not be made to endure losses sustained at the hand of management. Just as being a responsible head of household requires looking out for the financial security of all members of the household, so too leaders need to provide some "insurance" as well as "assurance" to enable members of the organization to survive worse-case scenarios.

Conversely, restricting rewards to those in leadership positions, along with other "high-potential" employees, concentrates a disproportionate amount of an organization's success in the hands of a precious few and discounts the efforts of members throughout the system. Programs like gainsharing, profit sharing, and other measurement-based systems provide a more equitable means for distributing wealth according to performance and value creation.

Alternative Pay Programs

To avoid the continued march to entitlement, smart managers are turning to the kinds of rewards systems we've just described. These "alternative pay" programs—as they're called—avoid additions to base pay, while focusing attention on performance. As a result, measurement-based payouts must be "re-earned" on a continuing basis, if employees are to realize a total reward experience that supports their needs and their wants. Moreover, if such awards are in the form of stock and stock options, their value is compounded in the marketplace over time.

Furthermore, such programs free managers from the dilemma of having to "lock" employees into specific niches to avoid having to change pay rates or to adjust employee pay for simply moving individuals from one area to another. In today's workplace, where flexibility and profitability are the name of the game, alternative pay programs allow employees to move about more freely and allow managers greater flexibility to adjust pay or not, as the case may be, according to individual performance and the value created.

As long as you as a manager continue to provide employees with opportunities to succeed and reward systems by which they can benefit, you will have gone a long way toward "building a better world" for everyone concerned.

Manager's Checklist for Chapter 10

❑ Concentrate on the right mix of base pay, benefits, and re-earnable incentives to provide employees with a total reward program that is competitive, fair, and measurement-based.

❑ Unlink performance planning and performance reviews from salary reviews. If the design of your reward system is objective and intelligible, employees will know what their rewards should be. Focus on development and the intrinsic value of doing meaningful work well.

❑ All work and no play make life in the new workplace pretty dull. Devise ways to have fun without insulting the intelligence of employees, who have enough sense to know if you're an authentic manager or a not-so-slick manipulator.

❑ Appreciate the value of distributing wealth equitably throughout the system. When everyone benefits, the organization as a whole gains immeasurably.

❑ Link the extrinsic value of rewards to the intrinsic value of the work. Having a larger view of what shared mission is all about will facilitate that process.

❑ Risk sharing and reward sharing are two faces of the same coin. Keep your employees educated, informed, and knowledgeable about what drives organizational success. If you're not "opening books" and enlarging views, someone may close the book on you and your organization.

The Reward of
Self-Actualization

The design team concluded its presentation to the board on the proposed reorganization of the agency. With such terms as "FTEs" and "strategic alignment," "job fragmentation," and "span norms," team members demonstrated how the "cents to manage an employee dollar" would be cut in half; how whole, integrated jobs would be undertaken by organizational members with minimum levels of supervision; and, for the first time in the history of the organization, how key human resources would be recognized as "process coordinators" and "professional resources" rather than department heads or area supervisors.

These same team members, who some eight months before had known little or nothing about organization design theory, strategic initiatives, profit and loss statements, or benchmarking, were now educating the board on the differences between data and information, marketing and community relations, and operational planning and strategic positioning. And, for the first time in their own history with the organization, each felt empowered to contribute ideas and suggestions to change their organization for the better.

As my colleague and I watched the "miracle" of transformation, we marveled at the even larger miracle of recovery and growth—almost half of the 10 team members had been homeless before coming to the agency and almost two-thirds had been chemically dependent and were now in recovery. As the doctors and professional board members listened, the confidence and authority with which members spoke and the command each exhibited over his or her subject matter overwhelmed them. Not only were team members focused on the proposed redesign, they were also advocating for involving other organizational members in the process of continuous redesign.

What was clear from the outset of the project was the need for a vision around "work"—what work would be appropriate for the future, which activities would add value, who would be responsible for what, how needed change would be incorporated into the ongoing process of continuous improvement. And, while the organization design project had given team members an opportunity to advance their own recommendations, in reality the emerging design was taking on an expression of who they were and who they wanted to become. No amount of incentives or compensation schemes could have motivated them to take hold of the project the way they had, nor could any outsider have had more insight into the ways in which the organization's work could be made more meaningful for all concerned.

A senior executive for a *Fortune* 500 company once remarked, "Work is not who you are, it's what you do." He was talking to an employee who was being fired, and it was his way of distancing the employee from the company and easing the pain of separation from what the employee had identified as his "career"—his work/life mission "on the job." But work is a

Work Expression

Smart Managing Just as no amount of money can offset the effects of poor supervision, no amount of pay can overcome the effects of bad job design and poor work content. Smart managers understand the thirst of the human spirit and the desire to find meaning at work—and in life. Because work represents the creative process by which individuals express themselves, both the content and structure of work need be aligned with the essence of what each person desires to do and is most capable of becoming. Smart managers are constantly aligning employee abilities with personal work/life goals.

creative expression of "self": it serves as an extension of our identity. If we're assigned to work that does not allow us the opportunity to "get into it" or "have fun" or express our real interests and abilities, then it is not aligned with who we are.

The remark of the senior executive certainly discounted the employee's view of himself and of his value to the organization, but it served to underscore the changed psychological contract between the company and employee. Reframing the executive's sentiment in the context of the new workplace, it might go more like "Don't confuse your personal work/life mission and your identity with who we are (the company or organization) and our identity." Smart managers appreciate the need to separate personal and organizational identities, but they also realize that they must know the talents and abilities of their employees and support their pursuit of personal work/life goals if they are to be truly recognizing of them.

> ## Aligning Views
>
> In a world of free agency and constant change, the reality is that recognizing the intrinsic value of work as a creative expression of self is more powerful than any single scheme or system of incentives. The challenge for smart managers lies in:
> - Restructuring work to be more meaningful to employees and more aligned with their personal work/life views;
> - Redesigning work to add more value to the organization;
> - Aligning individual effort and organizational goals in ways that fulfill the shared expectations of employees, owners, and customers.

Personal Appreciation

If recognition is a "whole person process," as we discussed in Chapter 6, and you're to be truly effective as a manager, you'll need to find more ways to express personal appreciation. As the workplace continues to change and diverse interests are brought to bear on satisfying organizational needs, managers will find the "standard" forms of personal recognition just won't work—if they ever did.

Consider the following example of a typical form of recognition that's obviously not working.

A manager expressed her surprise and anger at the attitude of one "elite group" of employees at her company. "We were preparing for a special event and needed volunteers to help with preparations. I went to each 'employee of the month' and spoke to them one on one, only to find that each and every one was not interested in staying after work or lending a hand outside their department. I thought, 'What kind of people has the organization been honoring and what qualities are being recognized, anyway?'"

Good questions—and the feelings were no more positive among the 'exemplary' employees. "I was embarrassed to be recognized as 'employee of the month,'" recalled one employee. "I didn't understand what I had done to deserve it, and it certainly didn't endear me to my coworkers."

More and more, traditional forms of recognition and appreciation are of questionable value. But we should be careful not to throw the baby out with the bath water. We need to accept that personal recognition is important but admit that the ways in which appreciation has been expressed in the past may not have been particularly meaningful. So, what does personal appreciation look like and why is it important?

In the new workplace, better forms of appreciation will be needed to address the individual and diverse needs of owned and contract employees. A one-size-fits-all approach will be far from effective—and certainly will not suit individual needs and diverse personalities and interests. Consider the following examples of smart approaches to recognition. (For the sake of simplicity, these examples are based on age groups, rather than individual differences.)

Older workers—once expected to be leaving the workforce at "retirement age"—are continuing on in allied positions to supplement income or retirement benefits in anticipation of longer life expectancy. Their values are such that they want to be appreciated for being "responsible" and "reliable" workers. Smart managers recognize these qualities and say, "Thank you for being so *responsible and reliable.*"

Xers need to see work as meaningful, personally and professionally, as we discussed earlier. Smart managers recognize the depth of their beliefs and say, "Thank you for *caring* so much about how we benefit others with the work we do."

Generation Y employees seek immediate payback and personal pleasure. Smart managers say, "Thank you for ensuring we provide *timely satisfaction* in all that we do."

The Net Generation seeks fast results, "virtual" solutions, and "intelligent" paybacks. Smart managers say, "Thank you for your *technical savvy*."

Free agents, especially those on the periphery of the workplace, seek opportunities to add value and to increase their own market worth. Smart managers say, "Thank you for *adding value*."

And, so it goes, with every interest in the workplace. Smart managers must recognize individual needs, interests, and abilities and find ways—not just in words but also in actions—to express personal appreciation for their people's separate and collective gifts.

People tend to value most appreciation that recognizes their individual progress toward self-actualization. When we recognize someone for extending beyond personal interest—by helping customers, by volunteering time for community initiatives, by putting the welfare of others ahead of his or her own—somehow we are honoring the larger person. We are recognizing service above self

---

Employee of the Millennium

Smart Managing

Care about every employee and recognize his or her personal interests. Avoid "standardizing" recognition, as with "employee of the millennium" approaches. Customize your appreciation. Value each and every employee with public expressions, personal appreciation, notes and letters, personalized mementos, special acknowledgments, new opportunities, different challenges, and so forth. Above all, avoid trivializing individual accomplishments by "punishing" employees with a dinner with the boss or privileges their peers will resent. If in doubt, ask someone who knows the individual well what he or she would appreciate. Smart managers care enough to do that little extra that says, "You're appreciated." And they know their real goal is to create an environment where all employees become "employees of the millennium."

and, in the process, we are raising that person's accomplishments to a higher level. In a word, we are catching individuals in the act of self-actualization—being all they can be, being larger than life, being above the crowd. And, it is in this vein that we are tapping into the intrinsic value of those individuals. We are acknowledging their contribution—their work—and, by extension, the creative expression of who they are, principally by focusing on the self-lessness of their endeavors.

Competition and Collaboration

So much has been written about teams and teamwork. However, we would be remiss here, in the context of self-awareness and self-actualization, if we did not focus on the value of collaboration and its inherent powers of recognition and reward. Let me begin with a story.

The staff had committed to an off-site retreat. It was an opportunity to get away and to deal with some of the substantive issues that had burdened their functional area for many months. Work demands were unending and the stress was almost intolerable.

As they sat around the table, an outside facilitator asked them to go through a pile of newspapers and magazines, cut out pictures that represented work for them, and glue the pictures to the front or the back of a large paper shopping bag. They went about the task quietly at first, then a little more exuberantly. When they were finished, the facilitator told them to find representations of leisure time—vacations, time away, etc.—and attach them to the opposite side. During this time, members were even more exuberant than before. Finally, the facilitator asked them to place inside the bag pictures and/or representations of personal stories, life events, private interests—perhaps unknown to the group as a whole.

At the conclusion of these activities, the facilitator asked members of the group to discuss the outside of their bags, beginning with their representations of work. As individuals began describing their scenes, all were struck with the similarity of depictions: battle scenes, pictures of crime victims, wreckage from storms or natural disasters. Indeed, "work" felt like one giant calamity or battleground; coworkers and bosses were viewed as "friends" or "foes." As they worked through the depictions of vacation and time away from work, common themes emerged around "calmness," "renewal," "re-creation": mountain lodges, seaside resorts, garden spots, parks, family outings, time with friends. The last stage of sharing centered around a facilitated disclosure of personal perspectives from inside the bag: secret longings, personal hurts, little-known information that illustrated the humanness and vulnerability of each member.

As the exercise concluded, the facilitator helped group participants see their shared perspectives and common goals. They no longer felt isolated, independent from others in the department; they now realized they could choose to work interdependently. Each resolved to collaborate with one another, not only to achieve the goals of the department but also to support the shared pursuit of personal goals.

That experience of a "combative" work environment is very similar to military experiences, where civilian strangers come together for the shared purpose of defeating the enemy before laying down their arms and returning to civilian life, going their separate ways. In today's workplace, savvy managers know they cannot keep the team together forever: assignments end, marketplace conditions change, "wars" conclude—and eventually all members will go their separate ways.

But, in the heat of "battle," savvy managers help team members see they are *competent*, *capable*, and *connected* in their shared experience of confronting some common "enemy" or in pursuit of some noble objective. And, truly great managers understand that the safety and welfare of their team is of the greatest importance if they are to "survive" and succeed in their mission. By recognizing employee needs and supporting their efforts, caring managers build confidence and foster superior results.

Collaborative efforts should be regenerative, as team members find ways to support one another and recognize both individual and group contributions. Needless to say, the training and

---

Collaboration vs. Competition

TRICKS OF THE TRADE Smart managers recognize that internal competition divides team members and impedes their ability to accomplish a larger mission. Smart managers:

- Facilitate understanding of shared goals and objectives
- Enable every team member to see how he or she is connected to the team
- Ensure understanding, to minimize disagreements and make agreements readily apparent
- Identify obstacles to team success and develops strategies to overcome them
- Recognize and reward team members individually and as a whole
- Keep group members aware of their primary mission

---

development of the team from the beginning is critical to ensure that regenerative skills become team competencies. Without training in teamwork, interpersonal skills, and problem-solving and continuous improvement techniques, project teams or other groups run the risk of missing the mark and ultimately self-destructing. Formed in the right way and with proper ongoing facilitation and support, teams and groups become self-recognizing and self-rewarding in their collaborative efforts and structures. Individual members feel appreciated by the team as a whole and each values, in turn, his or her teammates. Smart managers invest significant time and attention to forming and training teams. They know it's an effective means for designing the process of self-recognition *into* the system.

Someone Else's Wants

Life is mostly froth and bubble, two things stand like stone:
Kindness in another's trouble, courage in your own.
  —Adam Lindsay Gordon, "Ye Wearie Wayfarer"

Smart managers encourage employees to recognize their own potential and to be confident in their ability to succeed—or to at least *try*. This approach obviates the need for complex systems of extrinsic rewards—and, by so doing, results are better over the long term. Moreover, a collaborative system of organized effort puts the focus on group recognition and group rewards rather than on fostering individual competition among peers and generating "win-lose" scenarios.

Interview employees who have been recognized and rewarded in the workplace and many will tell you they could have done without. Certainly, that was what Tom realized when his regional boss flew into town to close his office. He asked, "What's to become of me?" The boss responded, "You've a wall full of plaques, we've paid you well, and we owe you nothing." Somewhere along the way Tom had bought the "froth." Now he knew that the real challenge would lie in having the courage to stand on his own. Today, he sells insurance to clients who value his services more than his former employer who paid him well and gave him plaques. His rewards are contracts and referrals from satisfied customers and his recognition comes from within himself and the knowledge that he's really good at what he does.

Smart managers encourage employees to:

- Stand on their own
- Value themselves and what they do
- Make needed changes in their work
- Pursue personal excellence
- Tap the resources of coworkers to grow and develop
- Learn continuously to increase their ability to change and adapt
- Be ready to jump—change assignments, jobs, careers
- Keep their options open
- View their career as a montage of experiences
- Value relationships, especially networks
- Appreciate managers who appreciate employees
- Continue to add value wherever they go

Adding Value

No one truly wants to feel or be perceived as "worthless"—even in the direst of circumstances. Perhaps one of the most powerful examples of this point comes from the writing of Viktor Frankl. In his book, *Man's Search for Meaning*, Frankl begins with a lengthy, austere, and deeply moving account of his imprisonment at Auschwitz and other concentration camps over a five-year period during World War II. It is the story of his struggle to find reasons to live.

Frankl posits that man should not ask what the meaning of his life is, but rather recognize that it is he who is called into question *by life*—he can only answer by being *responsible*. Ultimately, Frankl envisions himself in front of live audiences lecturing on the subject of the Holocaust, and it is his will to realize this vision—completing the "yet to do" task—that sustains him in his struggle for existence.

Each of us searches for some purpose in life, some reason for being. Curiously enough, when we envision ourselves "adding value" or "making a difference" or being "responsible," it's usually in the context of connecting with others. And it's precisely at that point that we get back what we've been missing; we get the answer to our question. Indeed, "adding value" is a vision of self-actualization and empowerment. It's not surprising that many people die soon after retirement; they see, in some sense, their "job" in life to be at an end. Others move on—perhaps into creative hobbies or into helping others, contributing to a larger life experience, and adding years of meaning and self-worth to their lives.

In the new workplace, a smart manager sees worth in others and works to help them see the worth in themselves. It is a process of encouraging the heart, as we discussed in Chapter 6. Smart managers are continuously reframing the work environment so others can see opportunities for adding value and understanding the value of their endeavors and, by extension, their own intrinsic worth. They're also reframing and redesigning work to align it with a vision of "adding value" and "making a difference."

Smart managers recognize and reward employees in the new workplace by enhancing their capacity to add value. Rewarding employees takes on different forms:

- Providing opportunities for employees to cross-train and expand their abilities
- Encouraging employees to learn as much as they can, continuously

Reframing The process of translating experiences, exchanges, or events into some "reasoned," even "transactional" view, so others can perceive the situation differently. Mediation is a form of reframing: it allows two, usually opposing parties to understand both sides of an issue and to see common ground. In today's new workplace, smart managers are constantly reframing so employees can see the value of what they do in a larger context—both personally and professionally. Reframing recognizes individual and team endeavors in a way that says, "You add value to this world—you make a difference."

- Delegating problem solving and decision making to employees, particularly in a team context
- Communicating the importance of their work and explaining its significance in the larger context
- Emphasizing the need to set personal goals and to develop a personal life mission
- Encouraging employees to move out of their comfort zone by trying new things—new programs, work assignments, projects, etc.
- Expressing appreciation for taking risks and making a difference by what they do

Adding value is a lifelong goal, one worthy of pursuit. As Frankl concluded, it is ultimately the act of taking responsibility. Smart managers understand that full well. They allow and even encourage employees to pursue the goal of being personally responsible *on the job*. In the context of work, to be accountable and to take responsibility is to be *empowered!* It's better than trinkets and more valuable than gold: enlightened managers recognize and reward employees by respecting their abilities and by allowing them the opportunity to add value—to be empowered.

In the Customers' Eyes

I've conducted hundreds of employee opinion surveys, and I'm always struck by how often employees say, "The reason I love my job is my customers" … "I'd have left long ago if it weren't for my patients" … "Taking care of my people (customers) is what keeps me going." Even when almost every other aspect of the job seems negative—and from time to time, that happens with every job—employees who decide to stay with an organization or an industry or a profession do so most often because of customers. And what employee doesn't appreciate a complimentary letter from a customer? It's that outside, personally interested, totally biased, sometimes tough to satisfy Customer (with a capital "C") who can recognize and reward like no other person.

Smart managers allow their employees freedom and authority to satisfy their customers. They understand, of course, that exceptional customer service is vital to the existence and viability of any organization. But they also understand—and here is a critical distinction—that allowing employees to satisfy customers is more than just good business: it's also one of the most powerful forms of recognition for employees.

Tricks of the Trade

Customer Feedback

Savvy managers solicit feedback from internal customers as well as from external customers. Not only does that practice help employees remember to treat other employees better with respect to their needs, but it also provides managers with an opportunity to acknowledge and recognize exceptional service within the organization as well.

Managers who understand these two important points empower their employees to provide excellent service and recognize them for doing so. They also ferret out any policies, practices, and structures that make it more difficult for employees to follow their instincts with respect to satisfying the customers. In addition, they promote heroic deeds and empowered ways of thinking, like managers at Federal Express, Southwest Airlines, Nordstrom's, and other organizations who encourage "out of box" thinking by employees to provide exceptional customer service.

Savvy managers learn to recognize employees through the customers' eyes, because customers can be not only the toughest critics, but also the best public relations representatives any organization could possibly want. And even though some businesses get by without great or even good customer service, studies have shown a high correlation between customer/employee satisfaction and total company profit.

Becoming a Free Agent

As we've indicated from the start of this book, free agency is the way of the future. And, just as corporations and other organizations develop mission and vision statements and set strategic goals and objectives, free agents need to do the same. Smart managers value their employees by seeing them as "free agents," regardless of whether they are owned or contract employees.

Oddly enough, the process by which individuals become free agents is the same process smart managers use for recognizing people for whom they have stewardship responsibility. Through personal performance planning, smart managers can engage employees in developing personal mission statements (what they are about "at work") and vision statements (where they want to be somewhere down the road). You can identify the major challenges for your organization or work unit and engage employees in a dialogue about how they want to be involved and ways in which they can contribute.

> ### A Chance to Contribute
>
> One unit manager decided to make employee turnover a "shared" concern. Rather than allowing her staff to engage in finger pointing ("Filling jobs is the employment manager's responsibility"), she asked each of them to consider what he or she could do to attract and retain employees. And, while it wasn't specifically in their job descriptions, everyone took on the responsibility and offered suggestions: develop a mentoring program, redesign orientation, improve training, be nicer to one another, etc.

Get employees to review their skills and to determine where they need to improve through learning, new experiences, and greater challenges. Have them assess their personal thinking

Thinking Larger
A smart manager finds ways to maximize resources. Make sure you're not underestimating the abilities and interests of your employees. Think "big picture," invite your employees to get involved, and help them stretch.

and behavioral style to determine environments in which they fit best. Have them identify the kinds of assignments they'd be willing to try, all things being equal.

Ask them what they'd change about their present areas of responsibility. Encourage them to identify others from whom they could learn desired skills. Find out what information or knowledge they could impart to others. Ask them what they would do to take care of themselves if the department were to "go out of business." In other words, have them view themselves as "free agents," getting ready to move out and take on new and challenging assignments.

Let's be frank: we all know there are things we could be doing differently at work, but rarely do we challenge ourselves to raise our heads above the piles of work to see where we should be going. In a world of uncertainty and rapid change, we can't afford to be caught with our heads buried in the pile. We all need to be reading the handwriting on the walls. Smart managers challenge employees to look at ways to add value every day, by eliminating redundant activities, outmoded practices, or little wanted services, or by doing something different. They recognize the ability of all people to make a difference—no matter what their title, income, or time on the job.

Manager's Checklist for Chapter 11

❑ Recognize that work is the creative expression of self. Work to align people's personal work/life vision with what they do in the workplace.

❑ Identify ways in which individuals and teams add value and express your appreciation in uniquely personal and appropriate ways.

❏ Understand that collaboration is a way of working that has regenerative powers of self-recognition. Foster collaboration rather than competition among employees.

❏ Empowering employees to satisfy customers is a powerful way of recognizing employees and building good business relations.

❏ Regarding employees as free agents enhances their growth and increases their capacity to add value.

Aligning Strategy and Rewards

If being "accountable and responsible" is a euphemism for "empowered," then it follows that *responsible* enterprises—those that also hold themselves *accountable*—are "empowered" and "empowering" organizations. Perhaps nothing is more telling of how responsible an organization is than the value system it actualizes on a daily basis. I make the distinction between "actualizes" and "espouses," because any number of organizations have put to paper their statement of values, but those that walk the talk are, indeed, responsible—and truly exceptional.

Responsible enterprises, enterprises that respect and value their resources, adopt and adhere to socially responsible policies. They protect the environment with processes that minimize waste and preserve our natural resources. They partner with communities in which they do business and they invest their time, talent, and treasure in ways that enhance social, human, and economic welfare. They honor their relationship with customers by producing products and services that are reliable, safe, responsive to personal needs, and "user friendly." They attract increased support from their investors and other key stakeholders by committing themselves to the endless process of reframing and renewal to ensure competitive viability and corporate vitality. And, they value employees—both "own" and "free agent"—with practices that dignify human life and evoke the creative potential that lies within each of us.

Responsible enterprises—and their managers—recognize and reward employees because it is appropriate to do so, particularly because their relationships should foster mutual trust and respect. Managers, especially, appreciate the grave responsibility they have to "make a difference" in the lives of others, and they assiduously develop and exhibit the quality of their leadership and their deepening commitment to the stewardship of the resources entrusted to them.

Responsible enterprises don't put managers in the untenable position of manipulating employees for profit. As one location manager put it, "I can't keep pushing my people to do more with less and all the while be stripping away their benefits. It's morally reprehensible." Responsible enterprises don't put managers in the untenable position of having to referee internal competition brought about by ill-conceived incentives and other gimmicks, when the name of the game should be collaboration and cooperation. Responsible enterprises don't put managers in the untenable position of concocting performance ratings

---

5 R's for Managing Responsibly

Smart Managing

Managing responsibly means:

- *Recognizing* employees in ways that contribute to their "independence"—as thinking, rationale, producing members of the work/life community;
- *Rewarding* employees fairly, equitably, and generously—consistent with the value they provide;
- *Reframing* problems, disappointments, and seemingly insurmountable barriers to success as "opportunities," "challenges," "solutions waiting to happen";
- *Redesigning and realigning* work activities continuously to do what is meaningful and avoid doing anything that wastes precious time and resources;
- *Realizing* how much managers don't know and how much employees can contribute to their mutual growth and development.

Companies Divided

Marsh Industries' CEO Rob Rodin eliminated individual incentives for 1,800 employees to stop internal bickering and competition. Instead, salaries were adjusted to keep people whole. "Our company was divided by internal promotions and contests.... We eliminated these distractions. Now we have collaboration and cooperation among (our) people." Many companies eliminated the traditional "Christmas bonus" in 1999 for a variety of reasons, not the least of which related to internal jealousies over bonus differences and the absence of any correlation between performance and discernable returns on "investment."
Source: Scott Hays, "Pros and Cons of Pay for Performance," *Workforce*, February 1999.

and meting out raises from increase "pools" that bear little or no relationship to individual and team results. Responsible enterprises don't put managers in the untenable position of being uninformed and unenlightened or of depriving others of important information. As another manager expressed it, "It doesn't matter whether we sit in the front of the plane or the back of the plane. If it's going down, it's going down, and we're all in it together."

Responsible enterprises view compensation as recompense for services rendered. Total reward strategies align with the interests of both the employers and the employees who commit their intellectual, physical, emotional, and spiritual capital on behalf of some ultimate Customer. Responsible enterprises view wealth accumulation as a resource to be shared equitably with all key stakeholders—employees, customers, investors, and employers.

To gain perspective on the value of employees, let me suggest that you ask entrepreneurs struggling to grow a business to prioritize the importance of their payables. You'll hear their *first* priority is "meeting payroll"—paying those who are doing the work—and *last* on the list is the owner. Indeed, more than one entrepreneur has had to forgo getting paid at one time or another, living on credit balances or personal savings until cash flow allows him or her to take money out of the pot. And in between are the "payables" that provide service to customers and keep them coming back. Next come the vendors and investors. Finally, as we've said, come the owners.

But, somewhere along the way, many enterprises turn this natural order of priorities or "payables" upside down: they put the owners first and add more "chiefs" to the process, with bigger salaries and even more overhead. And, when times get tough or the clamor for higher earnings becomes deafening, the first line of "expense" to be deferred or cut is payroll—more pointedly, employees who deliver services directly to the customer.

That's not responsible management. Responsible enterprises keep their priorities in order by balancing the needs of employees and the demands of the organization.

Business annals are replete with examples of CEOs and managers who have taken responsible care of their relationships with employees, only to be rewarded many times over. In the new workplace, I submit that one of the greatest challenges for managers will be to improve relationships with employees and practice responsible management as evidenced by respectful and responsible recognition and reward systems.

> ### The Cowboy's Rule
> **Smart Managing**
>
> Growing up in the West, I was told, "Smart cowboys take care of their horses." No matter how hungry, tired, or hurried the cowboy might be, the horse comes first. "Feed him. Rest him. Take good care of him." The idea was simple. If you were in trouble or in need, a horse in good condition could get you to where you needed to go—fast. Adapted to today's workplace, "A smart manager pays people appropriately, doesn't burn them out, and keeps them trained, informed, well-equipped. In turn, they get the organization to where it needs to go—just in time."

Aligning Strategy, Structure, and Systems

Approximately 75% of American business is still not aligned with its key strategies and objectives. Inefficient organization structures, restricted technology applications, outdated work processes, and poor people practices are systematically robbing organizations of their full potential. This realization by American business brought about massive reengineering initiatives, particularly in the 1980s and '90s, that contributed to huge layoffs and worker dislocation—a process that continues with the new millennium. And, yet these large-scale layoffs have not always brought about the desired results—usually expressed in financial terms—as almost half the companies have come to discover, according to *The Wall Street Journal* and other sources. For the most part, these companies have been "cutting expenses" rather than "increasing alignment." And, having done it once, they usually do it again.

As we continue to seek increased alignment in the new workplace, smart managers will have ample opportunity to make significant contributions. These will come in the form of:

Structure. Most assuredly, smart managers will work in partnership with employees to make work more meaningful and eliminate redundant, non-value-adding activities.

Strategy. Identifying the key strategies of any organization is critical to the process of giving *focus* and *clarity* to its members.

Commitment. As a result of all the downsizing and worker dislocations, we have been not only creating "free agents"—that's not all bad—but also generating indifference, apathy, and anger—and that's not good. Reengaging the spirit of commitment and collaboration will be a challenge. It will require the forging of new psychological contracts and work agreements with employees.* Indeed, in the new workplace, your role as manager will become even more important rather than less.

Recognition and Rewards. As smart managers look to the most effective ways to encourage commitment, they will need to devise recognition and reward *strategies* and *processes* predicated upon the shared interests for both their employees and their enterprises. Total reward systems will have to be developed to encompass all elements of recognition and compensation—direct and indirect, formal and informal—and will need to target the same outcomes as those of the organization.

*For more on this, check R. Brayton Bowen et al., *Anger in the Workplace: Losing the Ties That Bind*, National Public Radio Partnership series, Louisville: WFPL Studios, 1999.

Strategic alignment is best achieved by "insiders" acting with enlightened self-interest and "outside" assistance—particularly in the beginning of a redesign initiative. It is a critical responsibility of management to provide overall direction for assessing and aligning organization structures with business strategy. But, it is the primary task of managers to continuously make comprehensive, objective evaluations of functions, activities, and the people resources needed to evolve new structures that improve human, technical, and financial performance.

Increased productivity through employee involvement and strategic redesign is imperative for many organizations—and an integrated approach to recognizing and rewarding employees goes hand in hand. One human resources manager reported:

> We restructured our entire organization—moving to team-based design structures and employee involvement concepts—only to find we could no longer operate with the old compensation structure. It had been designed by a prominent consulting firm to control pay practices based on discrete, finite job elements. Today, we operate with whole, fully integrated work *processes* that no longer fit the old cookie-cutter approach to managing pay. We had to work with our structural design consultant to design new recognition systems and reward strategies that support the new structures and our overall mission. Both undertakings have made a huge difference in our being able to attract and retain employees.

Strategic alignment A term that we use for a condition wherein 80% to 90% of the work and related activities performed by the members of an organization are "value-adding" and directly associated with the primary mission of the organization. For example, marketing activities are value-adding for a marketing firm; healing activities, for health care; and manufacturing activities, for a producer of goods. In contrast, accounting activities are secondary activities for most firms, except for accounting firms, where accounting is the principal business. Management is a secondary activity, except in contract management firms, where managing contract labor is primary.

What Have You Done for Me Lately?

Be careful not to imply in any reward system the question, "What have you done for me lately?" This orientation only serves to distance employees from the organization and work against the best interests of all concerned. Everyone recognizes we get paid because someone expects us to do a job. But the "what-have-you-done-for-me-lately?" (WHYDFML) approach is not only offensive; it's also restrictive, belittling, and counterproductive.

Visions, Values, and Actions

It's difficult to be a dissenter when the prevailing "wisdom" shouts, "This is the way!" It's difficult to be alone in the wilderness when everything within you wants so desperately to be with others and be accepted. It's difficult to say "yes" to a course of action when all your experience and intuition say, "This is wrong." What guides anyone through such circumstances is an unwavering—though sometimes precarious—belief in a set of values or adherence to a vision or principle that allows us to be true to ourselves when, seemingly, everyone and everything is screaming, "Heretic!"

In today's workplace, this is the prevailing "wisdom" with respect to people and rewards:

- "Incentives motivate people."
- "If you pay people right, you can get them to do anything."
- "There's a 'right' reward formula for your employees."
- "People can't be trusted."
- "Pay (only) for performance."
- "You get what you pay for."
- "Today's help isn't very good."
- "Most people are lazy."
- "Foreign labor is cheaper than domestic (U.S.) labor."
- "Older people aren't flexible."
- "Employees, in general, just don't care."
- "No one really wants to work."
- "Someone who's been downsized can't be very good."
- "Only employed people are worth recruiting."

Small wonder that apathy, confusion, indifference, and anger abound in the workplace and that smart managers run the risk of being called "heretics" for believing in people and thinking everyone can be "productive" and "make a difference." We believe there are at least five critical factors in making a recognition and reward system successful:

1. The "vision" of any pay program must be formulated on the fundamental principle of *trust.*

2. Rewards must be viewed holistically—including fixed and variable pay components, formal and informal rewards, benefits programs, and the contextual situations in which such programs operate.

3. A total reward program or pay strategy must align with the mission of the organization.

4. Accumulated gains must be distributed appropriately.

5. A recognition and rewards system should be virtually invisible—totally natural.

Smart managers align the strategies of their recognition and reward systems—formal and informal, intrinsic and extrinsic—with the expressed vision, mission, and values of the organization. Consider the table on page 222, which illustrates that correlation.

Integrating "Doing," "Thinking," and "Feeling"

Effective reward strategies incorporate both personal and professional objectives and link them to corporate goals. Effective reward strategies recognize both individual and collective differences and encourage optimizing those differences. With respect to corporate performance specifically, effective reward strategies measure to some reasonable degree the following three things:

- The "doing" that goes on in organizations: task completion, achievement of performance goals, primary activities, core processes, etc.;

If the organization's vision is:	Then the system must:
• Overarching and "big picture"	• Appeal to the fulfillment of the larger view.

If the organization's mission is:	Then the system must:
• Purposeful and aligned with the vision	• Focus attention on "mission" work and value-adding core processes.

If the organization's values are:	Then the system must:
• Teamwork and collaboration	• Recognize interpersonal effectiveness, partnering, cooperation, collaboration.
• Innovation	• Support prudent risk-taking.
• Resourcefulness	• Reward problem-solving abilities.
• Competence	• Recognize and reward increased knowledge.
• Productivity	• Reward performance contribution.
• Customer satisfaction	• Empower and reward service excellence.
• Quality products and services	• Recognize and reward continuous improvement.
• Integrity and forthrightness	• Keep basically "honest" people honest.
• Financial performance	• Share gains equitably and generously.

Aligning strategies of recognition and reward systems with vision, mission, and values

- The "thinking" that happens and the "knowledge" that accumulates over time—that stuff called "intellectual capital," "skills," "competencies," or just "smarts";
- The "feelings"—yes, that's right, the stuff that's now referred to as "emotional capital." If you have any doubt about the importance of the latter, just take a good look at the way FTD florists promote their products the next time you need to remember a special occasion. They

appeal to customers to make someone happy, to brighten their day, to "say it with flowers." Consider Hallmark—its whole marketing appeal is based on emotion—"When you care enough to send the very best." And, their marketing cameos tell "emotion-filled" stories about caring and connecting with others.

Smart managers know that reward and recognition systems that empower employees focus on the "whole person"—*thoughts*, *actions*, and *feelings*—and their personal actions support all aspects of personal being. They recognize that to pay employees just to perform *tasks*—however narrowly or broadly they may be defined—is limiting. They must recognize interpersonal qualities, such as teamwork, cooperation, company spirit, positive demeanors, "can-do" attitudes. They must recognize the personal touches that make a difference, the attention to detail or the extra effort that increases customer satisfaction or improves quality of care.

Smart managers know that if they concentrate only on *numbers*—"tasks completed," "widgets manufactured," "products sold"—without addressing the qualitative aspects of *thinking* and *feeling*, they'll miss some very critical factors that contribute to overall performance.

Recognition and reward systems must address the triadic equation of "thinking," "doing," and "feeling" if they are to be "whole." The example of SRC is exceptional—not so much because of any "technique," like "opening the books," but because of *trust*. The culture of Southwest Airlines may be

> ### Encourage the Right Behaviors
>
> **⚠ CAUTION!**
>
> Numerous corporations and other organizations have been embarrassed by stories of executive bribes or money "under the table" or favors promised to win contracts or other business concessions—all in the name of "making the numbers." And numerous employees have held sales from one month to the next or "dummied" their transactions—all in the game of "looking good." Smart managers avoid programs that prompt basically honest people to do dishonest deeds.

> ### "Hard" and "Soft"
> Whether implementing a new employee recognition program or revising the old, consider "hard" and "soft" aspects:
> - *Symbols, rituals, and ceremonies.* Look at what should be continued. Consider how employees and the organization will benefit from the new forms of recognition.
> - *Traditions.* Preserve the best, invent the rest.
> - *Reward allocation.* Determine the optimum "mix" of fixed and variable pay components.
> - *Alignment.* Ensure that the new system aligns with the organization's strategic imperatives.
> - *Emotional quotient.* Determine what appeals to employees and how best to improve the emotional buy-in going forward.

regarded by some as a "cult"—but it's exceptional because of the *esteem* in which the leaders holds the employees. Levi Strauss may have been forced to yield to the pressures of globalization, but its reputation stands for *fairness* in dealing with employees. Toyota Motor Manufacturing may recognize and reward team members for their ideas, but it emphasizes *competence, innovation,* and *teamwork*, not incentive payments. Mary Kay Cosmetics may reward outstanding performers with pink Cadillacs and other perks, but the emphasis is on helping women build *self-esteem* and *independence*. In the end, it's the integrity of the system and not its mechanics that influences employees to feel motivated or not.

Build Responsibly: The Rewards Will Follow

The key to any good system is a good foundation. As one manager commented, "You can make almost any system work, but not every system works necessarily the way you make it."

This comment underscores the importance of the philosophy on which a reward system is predicated. All too often managers get hung up with structure or design of a program before they've tested the concept or determined the planned and unplanned results. The best way to avoid being disappointed is to build *responsibly* on a good philosophical foundation.

Integrative Management

Smart managers devote time and attention to integrating employee interests with organizational goals. Smart managers:
• Respect the need for employees to realize their own dreams.
• Value personal desires to improve.
• Respect people at any level of organization, life stage, or pay status.
• Recognize and celebrate the achievement of individual goals and personal milestones, including births, weddings, graduations—the hallmarks of personal and family life.
• Link personal goals to organizational needs.
• Recognize and reward individual and team progress and accomplishments.
• Even cry and laugh in empathizing, philosophizing, and recognizing work and life events.

For example, Max De Pree introduced the Scanlon Plan—a gainsharing program—to Herman Miller employees in 1950 not to get them motivated but to get "an owner and an employee in *every* position." (*Leadership Is an Art*, p. 97)

During the 1970s, General Motors owned almost half of the American car market. But by the end of the 1980s GM's market share had declined and Ford Motor Company's earnings had surpassed GM's. During this period, GM's Saturn project emerged—supposedly as a venture into technology and automotive robotics, but the management team at Saturn decided that "better people management" was more important than new technology. They created a "nonbureaucratic environment that set new standards in enlightened relationships with employees"—and the rest is history, as a new chapter opened in the life of GM.*

Actually, the path taken by Saturn's management was a departure from CEO Roger Smith's vision of the new factory at GM. In a word, it was a "mistake"—just like those we talked about in Chapter 3. In the Saturn project, employees were to be "de-emphasized," subordinated by the process. But the managers, by building responsibly and involving employees, created

*Lee G. Bolman and Terrence E. Deal, *Reframing Organizations* (San Francisco: Jossey-Bass Publishers, 1997), p. 4.

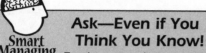

Smart Managing

Ask—Even if You Think You Know!

Employee involvement is fundamental to the concept of recognition, as we've said earlier. Don't be afraid to ask employees for opinions—even if you think you know the answer. There are at least three views to every process in your operation—how you *think* things are done, how they *actually* are done, and how you and your employees would *like* them to be. Building responsibly requires employee involvement.

a culture of recognition—in the form of human dignity, trust, and respect—that resulted in a resounding "win-win" for GM and employees. Saturn still operates in the larger context of GM and corporate GM management has periodically attempted to wrest control and risk the success of Saturn by reverting to traditional management practices. By staying the course, the corporation has gained more than not.

Savvy managers know that reward and recognition systems are just that: they're *systems* and as such have "shelf life," strengths, weaknesses, pluses, minuses. And it's essential for you, as a manager, to assess—constantly, objectively, whole-heartedly—whether the system you have in place is working in the best interest of customers, company, investors, and employees alike. Building—and rebuilding—a system responsibly and holistically is the best way to ensure rewards and recognition that meet the needs of all concerned.

Spend Time on What You Value—This Must Be Kansas

As we said earlier, if we can, we spend time with what we love. In life and work, time is too dear *not* to spend it on what we literally *love* and, ultimately, *value*. We hear of people who are *passionate* about what they do. They speak *passionately* about some cause or have some *passion* that is insatiable. These are people who *value* and *love* what they're about!

So much of what we've been about in the workplace in recent years, particularly in the United States—downsizing, globalizing, doing more with less—has been driven by legitimate

business concerns and conditions. I accept that when key decision makers have made such decisions they've done so believing they've had the best interests of their organizations and key
stakeholders in mind. But in the process we've lost the passion
of what we're about at work. And now more than ever, managers—*smart* managers, *savvy* managers, *passionate* managers—are needed to recognize and reward passion at work. In
the words of Max De Pree:

> Many managers are concerned about their style. They
> wonder whether they are perceived as open or autocratic
> or participative. As practice is to policy, so style is to
> belief. Style is merely a consequence of what we believe,
> of what is in our hearts. (*The Art of Leadership*, pp. 26-27)

New convenants, new contracts, new relationships are being
forged in the U.S. workplace, as we speak. As you minister to
the needs of people—customers, employees, the community at
large—choose work that adds value. Choose people who love
what they do. View their work efforts as expressions of who they
are. Implement recognition and reward processes that build
trusting relationships and value individual and group self-
esteem. Have confidence in people to do the right thing.
Recognize initiative and value progress as much as perfection.

Remember: pay is not a motivator. And, yes, you will be con-
sidered heretical in taking this position, but you will be in good
company of wise and learned thinkers and business people.
Competitive reward systems—simply and purely—spawn winners
and losers. The goal should be for everyone to be a winner.
Competitive award systems naturally breed competition, the
antithesis of collaboration—and, at best, they influence no one to
do more than they otherwise would be inclined to do. We need
systems that promote partnership, cooperation, mutual respect.
Systems of gainsharing, profit sharing, and open-book management move us in that direction. But, more than rewards, *recognition* is first and foremost.

Plenty of employees and free agents willingly invest themselves in organizations that don't pay the most. They do so

because they're appreciated and valued in ways that are personally meaningful. Go ahead and pay for performance, but do so *after the fact*—plan for it, root for it, shoot for it, but don't barter for it, manipulate and dominate others for it, or use and abuse employees striving for it.

Invest of *yourself*. As a manager, it's the most differentiating gift you bring to the table! And, in a relational context, it's the most powerful asset you own. Love what you do. Know who you are. Spend time with what you value, and honor the diverse and resplendent gifts each of us brings to the creative process of work. As we've transitioned from an agrarian to an industrial and from a post-industrial to now a virtual and technology-driven society, we must challenge the great temptation to become "faceless" and "emotionless" to others in a world of e-mail and e-commerce.

Recognition will become even more important as a means to express mutual awareness and respect. What you recognize and what you reward will be of vital importance—to you, to your employees, and to our collective future. It will be easy to hide behind an illusion, like the invisible and great Wizard of Oz, but in the end we must come out from behind the curtain and touch the lives of others. We must ensure that each among us knows, feels, and acts in ways that are reflective of a larger truth: that we are all competent, capable, and connected—*amuntu abuntu aganta*.

Manager's Checklist for Chapter 12

❏ Recognize and reward employees in ways that foster collaboration and cooperation.

❏ Balance the demands of your organization and the needs your employees. (Obviously, that's not always easy!)

❏ Ensure that work activities and work processes are aligned with the primary goals of the organization. Team up with employees to eliminate redundant and non-value-adding work.

❏ Constantly reframe work initiatives within the context of the organization's mission and major strategies to ensure that all employees understand and commit completely.

❏ Ensure that your reward strategies are integrated and holistically address all aspects of performance, including emotional and intellectual.

❏ Establish a sound philosophical basis and good motives for your reward and recognition process, to make it respectful and constructive in every way possible.

Bibliography

Peter Block, *The Empowered Manager* (San Francisco: Jossey-Bass Publishers, 1991)

Peter Block, *Stewardship: Choosing Service over Self-Interest* (San Francisco: Berrett-Koehler Publishers, 1996)

Lee G. Bolman and Terrence E. Deal, *Reframing Organizations* (San Francisco: Jossey-Bass Publishers, 1997)

R. Brayton Bowen, *Anger in the Workplace: Losing the Ties that Bind*, National Public Radio Partnership series (Louisville: WFPL Studios, 1999)

Alan Briskin, *The Stirring of Soul in the Workplace* (San Francisco: Berrett-Koehler Publishers, 1998)

Tom Brown, "Ringing up Intellectual Capital," *Management Review*, January 1998

Bill Capodagli and Lynn Jackson, *The Disney Way: Harnessing the Management Secrets of Disney in Your Company* (New York: McGraw-Hill, 1998)

Max De Pree, *Leadership Is an Art* (New York: Dell Publishing, 1989)

Peter F. Drucker, *Management Challenges for the 21st Century* (New York: HarperBusiness, 1999)

Martha Finney and Deborah Dasch, *Find Your Calling, Love Your Life* (New York: Simon & Schuster, 1998)

Viktor E. Frankl, *Man's Search for Meaning* (Boston: Houghton Mifflin, 2000)

Beverly Goldberg, *Age Works: What Corporate America Must Do to Survive the Graying of the Workforce* (New York: The Free Press, 2000)

Susan B. Gould, Kerry J. Weiner, and Barbara R. Levin, *Free Agents: People and Organizations Creating a New Working Community* (San Francisco: Jossey-Bass Publishers, 1997)

Cliff Hakim, *We Are All Self-Employed: The New Social Contract for Working in a Changed World* (San Francisco: Berrett-Koehler Publishers, 1994)

Douglas T. Hall and Associates, *The Career Is Dead: Long Live the Career* (San Francisco: Jossey-Bass Publishers, 1996)

Scott Hays, "American Express Taps into the Power of Emotional Intelligence," *Workforce*, July 1999

Scott Hays, "Pros & Cons of Pay for Performance," *Workforce*, February 1999

Frederick Herzberg, "One More Time: How Do You Motivate Employees?" *Harvard Business Review*, January-February 1968

Larry Hirschhorn and Thomas Gilmore, "The New Boundaries of the 'Boundaryless' Company," *Harvard Business Review*, May-June 1992

Michele Hunt, *DreamMakers: Putting Vision and Values to Work* (Palo Alto, CA: Davies-Black Publishing, 1998)

Richard W. Judy and Carol D'Amico, *Workforce 2020* (Indianapolis: Hudson Institute, 1997)

Kepner-Tregoe, *People and Their Jobs: What's Real, What's Rhetoric?* (Princeton, NJ: Kepner-Tregoe, 1995)

Alfie Kohn, *Punished by Rewards: The Trouble with Gold Stars, Incentive Plans, A's, Praise, and Other Bribes* (Boston: Houghton Mifflin, 1993)

James M. Kouzes, Barry Z. Posner, Tom Peters, *Credibility: How Leaders Gain and Lose It, Why People Demand It* (San Francisco: Jossey-Bass Publishers, 1993)

James M. Kouzes and Barry Z. Posner, *Encouraging the Heart: A Leader's Guide to Rewarding and Recognizing Others* (San Francisco: Jossey-Bass Publishers, 1999)

Abraham H. Maslow and Richard Lowry (editor), *Toward a Psychology of Being* (New York: John Wiley & Sons, 1998)

Jerry L. McAdams, *The Reward Plan Advantage* (San Francisco: Jossey-Bass Publishers, 1996)

Richard B. McKenzie and Dwight R. Lee, *Managing Through Incentives* (New York: Oxford University Press, 1998)

Haig R. Nalbantian and Andres Schotter, "Productivity under Group Incentives: An Experimental Study," *American Economic Review*, Vol. 87, No. 3, June, 1997

Bob Nelson, *1001 Ways to Reward Employees* (New York: Workman Publishing, 1994)

M. Scott Peck, *The Road Less Traveled* (New York: Simon & Schuster, 1998)

Jeffery Pfeffer, *Competitive Advantage Through People: Unleashing the Power of the Work Force* (Boston: Harvard Business School, 1994)

Jeffery Pfeffer, *The Human Equation: Building Profits by Putting People First* (Boston: Harvard Business School, 1998)

Donald Tapscott, *Growing up Digital: The Rise of the Net Generation* (New York: McGraw-Hill, 1998)

Patricia K. Zingheim and Jay R. Schuster, *Pay People Right: Breakthrough Reward Strategies to Create Great Companies* (San Francisco: Jossey-Bass Publishers, 2000)

Index